Fireworks & Festivals

Fireworks & Festivals

U.S. Holidays and Culture for English Language Learners

GRETCHEN FUES

North Seattle Community College
School of Teaching ESL

Ann Arbor
University of Michigan Press

Grateful Acknowledgments is given to those organizations for permission to print these photos.

Library of Congress for photo on pages 21, 95, and 112.

Thinkstock Images for most photos.

The University of Michigan Athletic Department for the photo on page 79.

ISBN-13: 978-0-472-03431-4

2016   2015   2014   2013   4   3   2   1

CONTENTS

To the Student

Who Is an American?

In this book, you will see the word *American*. This can be confusing. The Americas include many countries. In this book, the word *American* is used to refer to a citizen of the United States of America.

Why Do You Need to Know about U.S. Holidays?

If you live in the U.S., you will experience about 30 holidays every year. You might be curious about the traditions of the holidays. Do you know why Americans celebrate these holidays? What do people do on these days? What do they say to one another? How can you participate?

Each unit in this book has two parts. The first part is about the holiday. The second part is about an American who has a important connection to the holiday. The readings in both parts will give you helpful and interesting information. You will practice a lot of vocabulary before the readings. Exercises will help you to practice and remember the new words. They will also help you to understand the readings.

Why Do You Need to Know about Important Americans?

Learning about the United States and who its people are requires more than just learning the language. You also should know something about the history and culture of the United States. One enjoyable way to do this is to study important people in history. Who do many Americans admire? Why do many Americans admire these people? If you learn the answer to these questions, then you will learn something about American values. You might agree with these values, or you might not. But it is important to try to understand them if you want to better understand Americans.

How Can You Improve Your Vocabulary?

When we encounter a new word in any language, we need to hear it or see it many times before we can learn it. The first time that we hear or see a new word, we might find out what it means. The next time we hear or see it, we will probably notice it and we might remember what it means. After we hear or see it several times, we might be able to use the word. We might say it in a conversation. We might write it in a school assignment. When this happens regularly, it means that we have learned it. The exercises in this textbook practice this step-by-step process. First, you will be introduced to a new word. Then you will learn what it means. After that, you will practice it several times in different and interesting ways. Next, you will read the words in the stories. Finally, you will use the word in your own sentences. By this time, the new word will start to become part of your memory, and you should be able to use it whenever you want.

In each unit of this book, you will practice 10 new words. These words will help you understand the readings better. They are common words that you will be able to use in everyday English. These words will help you understand and talk about life in the United States. They will help you understand and talk about American people and history. They will help you understand and talk about American culture and values. To learn all of these new words, there are several things that you can do.

1. Complete the exercises carefully.

2. When you read the stories in this book, don't just read them one time. Read each story two or even three times. Reading the same text several times will help you understand the words.

3. Keep a vocabulary journal of all the new words that you learn. Write any new words in your journal that you learn from reading this book and doing the exercises. Write a definition or a translation of each new word and write it in a sentence. You could also write what part of speech it is. Is it a noun? Is it a verb? This information will help you know where it goes in a sentence.

4. Notice the new words as you see them. Pay attention to how they are different from words that you already know. Use the new words in conversations, in your homework, and in your writing. Practice the new words again and again. You will find that your vocabulary is growing. You will be able to understand and express more ideas.

Have fun with the readings and exercises here. You probably already know more than you think about the ideas in this book. Think about your own experiences in life. Think about the holidays in your family's native country. Think about its heroes. Think about what you might already know about North American holidays and heroes. Use this information when you answer the questions in this book.

I hope that *Fireworks and Festivals* is fun and interesting for you. Good luck as you continue to learn this challenging and fascinating language.

To the Teacher

Audience

This book was written for intermediate-level English language learners in high schools, IEPs, community-based organizations, or community colleges who wish to improve their vocabulary and better understand some of the history, culture, traditions, and heroes of the United States. This book may also be useful in standards-based programs that encourage critical thinking, reflection, and reading with understanding. It also promotes education in civics.

Reading and Writing Levels

Each unit is equal in its level of difficulty. Therefore, each unit can stand alone, and the units can be covered in any order. The readings are carefully controlled for length as well as difficulty of grammar and vocabulary. Each reading is approximately 500 words long and scores about 5.5 on the Flesch-Kincaid reading level scale. Grammatical structures include the simple tenses, the present and past continuous, the present perfect, and occasionally the past perfect, placing the text roughly at ESL reading and writing Level 4 (or intermediate level), as defined by the American Council on the Teaching of Foreign Languages (ACTFL) proficiency guidelines.

Vocabulary

This text offers students the chance to encounter new vocabulary many times, from noticing to remembering, to producing it independently. Thought-provoking readings and carefully designed exercises keep students motivated to learn and practice new vocabulary.

Each unit consists of two parts. The first half presents the history and present-day customs of a major U.S. holiday. The second half features the biography of a famous American who has a connection to the holiday. Each half unit features five target words. These high-frequency words are central to the reading. First, the new words are introduced with their definitions as related to the context of the reading and are highlighted in a sentence. Word families are included to further broaden students' vocabulary base. These words are each recycled and practiced throughout that half of the unit through a variety of engaging exercises, moving from controlled to free practice.

The highlighted words in the first half of the unit also reappear in the second half of the unit for reinforcement. Words are reinforced methodically throughout the book if the chapters are used in the order presented here. However, teachers can start the book anywhere because each unit can stand alone in terms of context and level.

U.S. Holidays and Select Biographies

Holidays are an engaging and natural way to involve language learners in U.S. civics, history, and culture. The history and values surrounding the holiday are highlighted by a biography of a historical figure who has a connection to the holiday. For example, New Year's Day becomes more interesting to students when they also learn about the New Year's tradition of American college football games and the great football player, Anthony Muñoz.

Learning about the kinds of people that Americans admire, what makes them significant in U.S. culture, and how they have influenced the culture helps students better understand some American values. In addition, students are asked to think about their own cultures and values. The holidays in this book were chosen to give students a varied look at U.S. history and its people, events, and values. The biographies selected represent a diverse range of American men and women, all of whom are honored or celebrated in U.S. society. Religious holidays were not selected, allowing the teacher to be sensitive to the faiths of students in the classroom.

Unit Format

Each unit features a high number of vocabulary-strengthening exercises that ask students their opinions and ideas on a number of subjects. In each half unit, students complete about 12 exercises: five before reading the text and seven after the reading. At the end of each unit, there is also an individual project for students to complete. This will extend the student's understanding of some of the concepts presented in the unit. Students can complete the exercises individually, in small groups, as whole group activities, or as individual homework assignments.

Each half unit follows the same format:

- **Think about the Reading.** Students activate their background knowledge and schema through discussion questions about the topic and holiday.

- **Practice New Vocabulary.** Students begin with carefully controlled vocabulary exercises such as cloze, circling parts of speech, making opinions, short answer, and noticing the words in context. Then they move to freer response exercises.

- **Read about It.** By now, the target vocabulary will have been circled by the students. Students then read the account of the holiday or famous American. For added authenticity, biographies end with a quote from or about that person. Students are given the opportunity to discuss with classmates what the quote means to them.

- **Check Your Comprehension.** After the first reading, students re-read the text. This is followed by a short self-test to check understanding. The holiday readings are followed by a true/false exercise, and the biography selections are followed by an exercise that directs students to make corrections to sentences. Both of these comprehension checks focus on the content of the readings.

- **Think and Discuss.** This section allows students to share their opinions and experiences with the whole class, a small group, or a partner, as the teacher chooses. While these questions do not all focus specifically on the material in the readings, students will have become attuned to the topic through their reading. In addition, students will think about the connection between the holiday and the famous American presented in the unit. These questions will give students the opportunity to strengthen their responses by using the unit vocabulary.

- **Write.** Here students extend their content and vocabulary knowledge by writing a short paragraph about the ideas in the unit. These writing exercises can be done in class or as homework, or they can be assigned to students who finish the other exercises ahead of the rest of the class.

- **Complete a Project**. At the end of each unit, students are provided the opportunity to ask an American his or her ideas about one of the concepts raised in the unit. Students will conduct a short interview and then compile the information into a report that can be presented orally and/or in writing. This meaningful extension exercise allows students to further reflect on the concepts and vocabulary presented in the unit.

Pre-UNIT

An Overview of U.S. Holidays

Think about the Reading: U.S. Holidays

- What are some things that people around the world celebrate?

- What are some of the holidays that people in your family's native country celebrate?

- What do you think you will learn in this book about American holidays and culture? What are some questions that you have about what Americans celebrate and how they celebrate?

Practice New Vocabulary before You Read

Target Vocabulary

A. Learn the Words

Read the definitions. Notice how the words are used in the sentences.

ancestor (n.)—a person in your family who died long before you were born.

> *I was born in the United States; my* **ancestors** *came to the United States from Germany in 1850.*

cemetery (n.)—land where people who have died are buried.

> *My family and I visit the* **cemetery** *where we buried my grandfather last year. We plant flowers there to keep it beautiful. It helps us to remember him.*

Congress (n.)—the group of people who represent the 50 American states. This group makes laws for the United States.

> *The two parts of* **Congress** *are called the Senate and the House of Representatives. People who work in the Senate are called Senators. People who work in the House of Representatives are called Representatives.*

culture (n.)—the kind of art, music, food, manners, and values that a society has.

> *The United States is a mixture of many different* **cultures***.*

The adjective form is **cultural**.

> *The* **cultural** *traditions of Irish-Americans have influenced the United States.*

custom (n.)—a specific habit or practice that a group of people share.

> *One* **custom** *in the U.S. is to shake hands with someone the first time you meet.*

The adjective form is **customary**.

> *It is* **customary** *for both men and women to shake hands the first time they meet.*

federal (adj.)—national; used to talk about the national government.

> **Federal** *taxes pay for things like roads, health programs, and the military.*

honor (v.)—to show high praise and appreciation for someone or something; to give an award to someone.

> *We **honor** people on their birthday. We can tell them how important they are to us.*

The noun form is spelled the same and is common.

> *It's an **honor** for me to be the guest speaker today.*

observe (v.)—to celebrate a holiday or ritual; to watch carefully.

> *My school **observes** several holidays during the year.* (This means that no one comes to schools on those days.)

parade (n.)—a procession where people march in an organized way.

> *One famous **parade** in the city of Seattle happens in the summer. It is called the Torchlight Parade. It begins in the evening. About 300,000 people go to watch. People march, bands play music, and dancers perform.*

tradition (n.)—thoughts, actions, stories, or beliefs, usually coming from older generations. This can be the same as "custom," or it can mean a much older practice.

> *One wedding **tradition** in many countries is for the woman to wear white.*

The adjective form of is **traditional**.

> *It is **traditional** for the man and woman to give each other wedding rings when they get married.*

Complete the paragraph with vocabulary words from the box. Be careful! You might need to change the form of the word. That means that you might need to make it plural or change the form of the verb ending.

ancestor	culture	honor	observe	tradition

On holidays in the U.S. today, Americans ① _____ important people, and remember religious and historical events. Americans ② _____ their holidays by doing something special. Different groups of people in the U.S. have different ③ _____, which means that their food, music, and even their languages might be different. Sometimes this is because their families or their ④ _____ came from other countries. This partly explains why there are so many different ⑤ _____ for the same holidays in the U.S.

Look at the sentences. The new words are underlined. Do the sentences make sense? Write yes if the sentence makes sense. Write no if the sentence does not make sense.

Example: My <u>ancestors</u> came to the U.S. from England last month. ___*no*___

1. A <u>custom</u> is something that nobody does. _____

2. <u>Congress</u> makes laws for the U.S. _____

3. A <u>federal</u> program is a program that only one or two states have. _____

4. People can be buried in a <u>cemetery</u> after they die. _____

5. A <u>parade</u> can have just one person. _____

> Now scan the reading on pages 7–8 for the target vocabulary words. You might find them more than once. Circle the words. Then compare your results with a partner. Did you both circle the same words?

B. Practice the Words

1. Read the sentences. Circle the number that reflects how much you agree or disagree. This is your opinion. Then compare your answers with a partner or group. Are your answers the same or different? Did you understand the vocabulary?

		agree		disagree		
a.	Parades are fun to watch.	1	2	3	4	5
b.	It's important to pay federal taxes in any country.	1	2	3	4	5
c.	In my family's native country, most people are buried in a cemetery when they die.	1	2	3	4	5
d.	Congress is more important than the President is.	1	2	3	4	5
e.	Everyone should honor his or her ancestors.	1	2	3	4	5
f.	I have friends from different cultures.	1	2	3	4	5
g.	Holiday customs in the U.S. are the same as in my family's native country.	1	2	3	4	5
h.	Old traditions are better than new traditions.	1	2	3	4	5
i.	My family's culture is similar to American culture.	1	2	3	4	5
j.	I can observe the holidays from my family's country in the U.S.	1	2	3	4	5

2. Complete the sentences. Then compare them with a partner. Talk about what you wrote.

a. People in my family's native country <u>observe</u> the New Year in the month of

_____.

b. One birthday <u>tradition</u> that my family has is _____.

c. In my family's native country, many people have the <u>custom</u> of

_____ when a baby is born.

d. One <u>federal</u> holiday in my family's native country is _____.

e. One thing that I love from my <u>culture</u> is _____.

3. Discuss these questions with a partner. Listen to each other and try to learn something new. There is no right or wrong answer.

a. How can people <u>honor</u> their parents?

b. Why do you think our <u>ancestors</u> are so important to us?

c. Are there <u>parades</u> in your family's native country? When?

d. How often do you go to the <u>cemetery</u>? Why do you go?

e. What is one law that you think <u>Congress</u> should make for the United States?

Read about It

Where Did Holidays Come From?

Throughout history, people have had a natural desire to celebrate. People want to honor the events that remind them of who they are. Native Americans were the first people who lived in North America. They arrived more than 10,000 years ago. They celebrated many things. They showed respect to the sun, the moon, and many gods. They remembered important battles. They honored their ancestors. They danced, sang, and prayed. They played instruments. They gave gifts. They shared traditional food.

In the 1600s, immigrants* began to come from Europe. They wanted a new life in a new land. They brought their traditions with them. Like the Native American's, they wanted to celebrate their cultures. They wanted to remember their histories. Today, America's holidays are a reflection of its people. These holidays tell a special story about important events or people in American history. They tell about the people who live in North America and who came from all over the world. Their histories are unique. Their ideas and customs are, too.

How Do Americans Celebrate Holidays Today in the U.S.?

There are about 30 holidays every year in the U.S. Ten of these are federal holidays. The U.S. Congress chooses which days will be federal holidays. Congress also decides when they will be observed. If a holiday is on a Sunday, it may be observed on a Monday. On federal holidays, most public offices are closed. Post offices are closed. Banks, government offices, and some schools are also closed. Most federal employees do not work on these days.

* immigrants—people who come to live in a new country

Private companies are different. They can choose whether they will close or stay open on holidays. Most of them observe the six biggest holidays. That means that they usually close on New Year's Day, Memorial Day, Independence Day, Labor Day, Thanksgiving, and Christmas. Most private companies stay open on the other four holidays. These holidays are Martin Luther King, Jr.'s Birthday, Washington's Birthday, Columbus Day, and Veterans' Day. There are about 20 other holidays that are not federal. They are cultural or religious. On these days, businesses and schools are usually open. Each state can decide which of these holidays to observe.

Each U.S. holiday has its own customs. Many traditions have been passed down from people who lived long ago. There are often firreworks* and public festivals. People spend time with their friends and family. Sometimes they give presents to one another. Sometimes they go to the cemetery. There is traditional food and music. There are parades. In the warmer months, people go on picnics. Stores have sales, and many people enjoy shopping.

Our holidays are important, no matter where we live. They help us remember the events from history that have shaped us. We can honor the traditions of our ancestors. In the U.S., people can observe holidays in different ways. They learn from the many cultures and have fun with the celebrations.

*fireworks—explosions of light and noise, usually set off to celebrate something

Check Your Comprehension

Read the story again. Write T for true or F for false.

1. Holidays were started in North America. _____

2. The Native Americans celebrated their culture. _____

3. Immigrants to the U.S. only celebrated the Native Americans' culture. _____

4. There are 30 federal holidays in the U.S. today. _____

5. Congress decides which holidays will be celebrated as federal holidays. _____

6. Everyone works on federal holidays. _____

7. No one works on cultural or religious holidays. _____

8. Labor Day is one of the biggest federal holidays in the U.S. _____

9. All 50 states today celebrate the same cultural or religious holidays. _____

10. American holidays have their own customs. _____

Think and Discuss

Work with a partner or group. Think about the reading. Discuss the questions. What do you think? What does your partner think? There is no right or wrong answer.

1. How do people in the U.S. celebrate holidays? Is this similar to or different from the ways people in your family's native country celebrate? Explain.

2. What is the name of one of your ancestors? Does your family have a special day to honor your ancestors?

3. Have you ever seen a parade in any country? Have you ever been in a parade? What was the occasion? Describe your experience.

4. In your family's native country, do you have both federal and cultural / religious holidays? Do schools close for all holidays? Which businesses stay open on these days?

5. Have you celebrated any holidays in the U.S.? How did you celebrate them?

Write

Choose one of the topics, and write a paragraph of at least 5–7 sentences on a separate piece of paper.

1. How many holidays are there in your family's native country? Which holidays are the biggest and most important ones? How do people celebrate?

2. What is your favorite holiday? Why is it your favorite? Who do you spend it with?

3. One of the themes of the reading is diversity. How is diversity reflected and celebrated in the U.S. holidays you know about? In your family's native country, are there any holidays that reflect or celebrate diversity?

UNIT 1

Labor Day and César Chavez

Think about the Reading: Labor Day

- Do people in your family's native country celebrate workers? When? How?

- How long is a typical work day in your family's native country? How long is a typical work week?

- What are some things that people in your family's native country do on weekends?

Practice New Vocabulary before You Read

Target Vocabulary

A. Learn the Words

Read the definitions. Notice how the words are used in sentences.

bargain (v.)—to try to reach an agreement through compromise.

> *If you want to **bargain** for a higher salary, you agree to work longer hours.*

The noun form is spelled the same.

> *The workers and the management team made a **bargain**.*

earn (v.)—to get something after working for it; to get money for doing a job.

> *I **earn** enough money to pay my rent.*

industry (n.)—companies or businesses of a certain type.

> *A company that makes cameras and a company that makes computers are both part of the electronics **industry**.*

Industry can also mean manufacturing in general.

> ***Industry** in Canada grew last year.*

union (n.)—an organization of workers, either in one company or in one type of business. This organization helps workers to have better worker safety and freedoms. This is only one meaning of this word.

> *My teachers' **union** argued for higher salary for all of the teachers at my school.* (This is often written as **labor union**; *labor* = work.)

wage (n.)—the money paid for doing a job, usually per hour, day, or week.

> *My **wages** are too low. I want a job that pays better.*

Complete the paragraph with words from the vocabulary list. Be careful! You might need to change the form of the word or change the verb ending.

Labor ① _____ in the United States are active in

professions like teaching, the police force, and the manufacturing

② _____. Union ③ _____

with the company for better working conditions. This

includes better working hours, health benefits, and

④ _____. Millions of people across the United

States ⑤ _____ a better living because of

unions.

Now scan the reading on pages 15–16 for the target vocabulary words. You might find them more than once. Circle the words. Then compare your results with a partner.

B. Practice the Words

1. Read the sentences. Circle the number that reflects how much you agree or disagree. This is your opinion. Then compare your answers with a partner or group. Are your answers the same or different? Did you understand the vocabulary?

		agree		disagree		
a.	I want to earn a high wage.	1	2	3	4	5
b.	The electronics industry is important to my country.	1	2	3	4	5
c.	A company with good managers doesn't need a union.	1	2	3	4	5
d.	Every worker should join a union.	1	2	3	4	5
e.	In my class, students can bargain with the teacher.	1	2	3	4	5
f.	Friendship is not a free gift. You must earn it.	1	2	3	4	5
g.	It's easy for me to bargain for low prices when I shop.	1	2	3	4	5
h.	A worker with more experience should earn higher wages.	1	2	3	4	5

2. Complete the sentences. Then compare them with a partner. Talk about what you wrote.

a. The minimum <u>wage</u> where I live is _____ an hour.

b. One <u>industry</u> where I live is _____.

c. I once <u>bargained</u> for _____.

d. One good thing that a <u>union</u> can give its members is

   _____.

e. I <u>earned</u> about $_____ per week at my first job.

Read about It

Labor Day

Labor Day is a different kind of American holiday. It is not a celebration of a famous person or a historical event. It does not honor any religion. People don't eat special foods on this day. No one gives or receives gifts. This holiday honors the workers in the United States. It is a day that recognizes their importance in history. Workers have helped make the U.S. industry strong.

In the 1800s, the U.S. had an Industrial Revolution. Many industries grew. Some of these industries were farming, manufacturing, and transportation. Factories* were built. Cities grew. The U.S. became rich, but many people were still poor. Working conditions were not good. Men and women often worked 12–14 hours a day. They did not have any days off. Many young children also worked all day. Wages were low and people could not earn enough money. Many factories were not safe. There were many accidents and deaths. Therefore, employees began to talk together. They formed groups to talk about their working conditions. These groups, or unions, became strong. They had many members. The union leaders could bargain with the management. Unions also went to Congress. They bargained for better working conditions.

In 1882, one union leader had an idea. Many people believe that this man was Peter J. McGuire. McGuire wanted to honor the men and women who work in this country. He thought the U.S. needed a special day to do that. He believed that such a day would show the country how important all workers are. A strong industry needed healthy, happy workers. He wanted management everywhere to understand that. He also wanted workers to feel proud of their work.

*factories—places that make things by machine that are sold

McGuire started a new holiday that September. He called it "Labor Day." On that day, there was a parade in New York. Ten thousand workers marched in the streets. Afterward, there was a huge picnic with speeches, dancing, and fireworks. This helped to bring a lot of attention to labor unions and their workers. Working conditions began to improve in some areas. The typical workday became eight hours long. People could take breaks and holidays. Child labor laws were passed. Wages increased. The workplace became cleaner and safer.

How Do Americans Celebrate Labor Day Today in the U.S.?

In 1887, Oregon was the first state to recognize Labor Day as a holiday. Six years later, Labor Day was celebrated in 30 states. Today, all 50 states celebrate this day. It is a federal holiday. Americans believe in the importance of hard work, which can lead to a better life. The connection to unions and workers is not as strong today as it was in the past. Labor Day is always on the first Monday in September. This gives workers a three-day weekend. It's a chance to enjoy the end of summer. Many people take vacations. There are also music festivals, parades, and art shows all over the country. In addition, many stores have sales. Thousands of people celebrate Labor Day by shopping.

Check Your Comprehension

Read the story again. Write T for true or F for false.

1. Labor Day was started to honor a famous person. _____

2. The Industrial Revolution happened in the 1800s. _____

3. The Industrial Revolution made the U.S. and its workers rich. _____

4. Unions bargained for better working conditions. _____

5. The work day was finally shortened to seven hours. _____

6. Peter J. McGuire was a member of Congress. _____

7. Labor Day is celebrated in September. _____

8. New York was the first state to officially recognize Labor Day. _____

9. Today, all 50 states in the U.S. recognize Labor Day. _____

10. Today, people celebrate Labor Day in many different ways. _____

Think and Discuss

Work with a partner or group. Think about the reading. Discuss the questions.

1. Why were labor unions needed in the U.S.?

2. Why did Labor Day become a holiday? Do you think this holiday was a good idea? Why or why not?

3. Do you know other countries with labor unions? Do you know other countries that celebrate a Labor Day?

4. In what ways are workers' rights protected or not protected in different parts of the world today?

5. Was there an Industrial Revolution in your family's native country? When?

Write

Choose one of the topics, and write a paragraph of at least 5–7 sentences on a separate sheet of paper.

1. Imagine you are a union leader in a specific industry today. What are the most important labor issues in your industry?

2. Think of one type of worker who makes a difference in your life. What does this person do? What is his or her job like?

3. Some people think it's important and necessary to belong to a union. Other people do not want to join. What do you think? What are some arguments for and against belonging to a union?

——————————————————— ★ ———————————————————

Think about the Reading: César Chavez

• What kinds of farms do you know about? What do they produce?

• What are some jobs on a farm? Are they easy or difficult? Why?

• Have you ever visited or worked on a farm? Describe your experience.

Practice New Vocabulary before You Read

Target Vocabulary

A. Learn the Words

Read the definitions. Notice how the words are used in sentences.

effective (adj.)—successful; something that works well.

> *My diet was **effective**! I lost 15 pounds.*

encourage (v.)—to support someone; to give someone hope, confidence, or courage.

> *A good teacher **encourages** his or her students when they have difficulty in a class.*

The noun form is **encouragement**.

> *Our soccer coach gave us a lot of **encouragement** when we lost the game.*

extremely (adv.)—a stronger word than *very*.

> *Be careful! That pan is **extremely** hot. Don't touch it!*

influential (adj.)—important or strong enough to change the way other people think or act.

> *People can be very **influential**, so it's important to choose your friends carefully.*

The verb form is **influence.**

> *My grandfather doesn't have much money, but he **influences** me to be generous in all situations. He tries to give money to anyone who has less than he does.*

praise (v.)—to say good things to people about themselves.

> *Managers should **praise** their workers when they do a good job.*

The noun form is spelled the same.

> *I was happy to receive the **praise** from my teacher about my test score.*

Choose the correct part of speech/word form for each word. Circle the correct answer.

1. This medicine is not (effective / effectively). I still have a headache!

2. Thank you for the (encourage / encouragement) when I lost my job.

3. A good education is (extreme / extremely) important if you want to get a good job.

4. An (influence / influential) person can make big changes in a company.

5. My mother often (praises / praise) me for cleaning my room.

Now scan the reading on pages 21–22 for the target vocabulary words. You might find them more than once. Circle the words. Then compare your results with a partner.

B. Practice the Words

1. Read the sentences. Write A if you agree, D if you disagree, and X if you can't decide. Then compare your answers with a group.

a. It's very important to praise young children often. _____

b. A person who earns high wages is extremely lucky. _____

c. Part of a teacher's job is to encourage every student. _____

d. Your parents are the most influential people in your life. _____

e. An effective manager is someone who is nice. _____

f. Praise is more important than money. _____

g. Everyone needs encouragement. _____

h. Teachers can influence students. _____

2. Discuss these questions with a partner.

a. What are some qualities of an <u>effective</u> worker? What are the qualities of an <u>effective</u> manager?

b. Talk about a time someone <u>praised</u> you. What did he/she say?

c. Who is an <u>influential</u> person in your life? Why?

d. What kinds of jobs do you think are <u>extremely</u> important to your country?

e. Imagine you want to <u>encourage</u> someone who failed a test. What would you say?

Read about It

Who Was César Chavez?

Labor Day was created by the leader of a union. Union leaders have been important in America's history. Another union leader was named César Chavez. He was born poor, but he became very influential. He worked hard for farm workers. He helped to organize them. He helped them to get union contracts. He gave them encouragement when the work was hard.

Courtesy Library of Congress

César Chavez was born in Arizona in 1927. His family lost their home during the Great Depression.* They moved to California because there were jobs for migrant farm workers there. The word *migrant* means moving from place to place. That is what migrant workers do. They travel from farm to farm, following the jobs. They don't work or live in the same place very long. When Chavez finished the eighth grade, he quit school. He began working with his family. They were migrant workers on many different orchards (where fruit grows) and farms.

Chavez found that life for migrant farm workers was very difficult. They did not have any protection from poor working conditions. They did not have many civil rights.* Hours were long, there were few safety measures, and wages were extremely low. Children worked as hard as adults. However, if workers complained, they could be fired.

* **Great Depression**—a period in the U.S. from 1929 through the 1930s when many people had no jobs and little money
* **civil rights**—protection of the freedom and safety of citizens

The workers did not have any power. They did not have a strong union or influential leader. They could not bargain for better conditions or complain. Chavez formed a union. It was called the National Farm Workers Association. In 1965, a group of Filipino workers began a strike when grape growers cut their wages. A *strike* is when workers decide to not work until the management makes changes. The two groups formed a new union. It was called the United Farm Workers (UFW).

Chavez was their leader, and he was extremely effective. He knew he needed the support of the American people. The union therefore asked the public to not buy grapes. This hurt the grape and wine industry. In 1966, UFW members went on a 25-day march. They walked across California and stopped at the state capital. This brought attention to the problem. People across the country were curious about the protest. In 1968, Chavez stopped eating for 25 days. He did this to influence people. He wanted them to notice what was happening. Dr. Martin Luther King, Jr., and Robert Kennedy encouraged Chavez. They praised his peaceful methods of protest. After five years, many grape growers agreed to improve conditions, and the strike ended. The growers signed a contract with the UFW. This contract gave members higher wages. Working conditions improved. Members got health insurance.

Chavez continued to fight for farm workers. He helped them fight for their civil rights. When he died, thousands of people came to his funeral. In 1994, President Bill Clinton praised Chavez' life work. He presented Chavez' wife with the Medal of Freedom. This is a high honor for people who help make the U.S. a better place.

> "It is possible to become discouraged about the injustice we see everywhere. But God did not promise us that the world would be humane and just. He gives us the gift of life and allows us to choose the way we will use our limited time on earth. It is an awesome opportunity." (César Chavez)

Check Your Comprehension

Read the story again. Then change the sentences to make them true.

Example: César Chavez was born in ~~California~~. *Arizona*

1. César Chavez moved to California before the Great Depression.

2. César Chavez' family owned a farm in California.

3. Life for migrants was comfortable because they had few civil rights.

4. If workers complained, they could be hired.

5. United Farm Workers was the name of a business.

6. Chavez was the secretary of the UFW.

7. The union asked the public not to grow grapes.

8. King and Kennedy praised Chavez for using violent methods to change conditions.

9. The strike against the grape owners began when the union members got a contract.

10. Chavez stopped working for workers' civil rights after the strike ended.

Think and Discuss

Work with a partner or group. Think about the reading. Discuss the questions.

1. Why was César Chavez a great American?

2. How can a strike help workers? How can a strike hurt workers?

3. Re-read the quote by César Chavez. What do you think he means? Do you agree that we have an "awesome opportunity" in this life? Why or why not?

Write

Choose one of the topics, and write a paragraph of at least 5–7 sentences on a separate piece of paper.

1. César Chavez was not born into an influential family. His family was not rich. They did not have much power. However, Chavez became an influential leader. How do you think that he did that? Do you think it was important that his family was not rich? What do you think it takes to be an influential person?

2. Are there migrant farm workers in your family's native country? What kinds of jobs do they do? How important are migrant farm workers to the farming industry there?

3. Think of one current fight for civil rights. What can people do to solve the problem? What can you personally do?

Complete a Project

How's Your Job?

1. You are going to interview someone in English about his or her job. Use this form. Ask the questions listed. (<u>Cultural note</u>: It is not polite to ask American workers how much money they make.)

What is your name? _____

What is your job? _____

What industry is your job in? _____

Do you like your job? Why / Why not? _____

_____

_____

Do you belong to a union? Why / Why not? _____

Name something that you like about your job. _____

_____

_____

_____

Name something that you don't like about your job. _____

_____

_____

_____

2. Prepare a short written report for your class. Explain what you learned about the person's job and working conditions. Would you recommend this job to your classmates? Why or why not? Write your report. Present your report to your class.

My report on an American worker's job:

_____

_____

_____

_____

_____

_____

_____

_____

_____

_____

UNIT 2

Columbus Day and Sacagawea

Think about the Reading: Columbus Day

- What do you know about the first people who lived in your family's native country? Who were they?

- Are there people from all over the world in your family's native country? Where are they from?

- What are some of the different groups of people in the United States? Where are they from?

Practice New Vocabulary before You Read

Target Vocabulary

A. Learn the Words

Read the definitions. Notice how the words are used in sentences.

admire (v.)—to respect someone or something very much.

> *I **admire** people who help others.*

The noun form is **admiration**.

> *I have a lot of **admiration** for people who help others.*

discover (v.)—to find new information about someone or something. This can also mean to find a new place.

> *I'm always happy when I **discover** new restaurants in my city.*

The noun form is **discovery**.

> *The **discovery** of penicillin helped to make infections less serious.*

explore (v.)—to go to new places and learn about the area or people.

> *I like to **explore** new places when I travel.*

The noun form is **explorer**.

> *An **explorer** is a person who likes to go to new places and learn information about those places.*

force (v.)—to make someone or something do something.

> *When we cross the street, I **force** my child to hold my hand. Sometimes she doesn't want to, but I make her do it.*

The noun form is the same.

> *When a thief wants to come into a house, he or she might try to open a window by **force**. (This means that the thief might use a tool to break the locks on the window.)*

trade (v.)—to buy, sell, or exchange goods and services.

> *When people come to the United States, they usually **trade** their country's money for dollars.*

The noun form is the same.

> ***Trade** between countries is an important part of the economy.*

Complete the paragraph with words from the vocabulary list. Be careful! You might need to change the form of the word or the verb ending.

I ① _____ people who like to ② _____

different cultures and learn about other countries. However, I can

always ③ _____ new things about myself and my own

beliefs when I leave my country. I think that all schools should

④ _____ their students to learn a new language and to

travel, and I think all students should learn about international

⑤ _____. Do you agree?

> Now scan the reading on pages 30–31 for the target vocabulary words. You might find them more than once. Circle the words. Then compare your results with a partner.

B. Practice the Words

1. Read the sentences. Circle the number that reflects how much you agree or disagree. This is your opinion. Then compare your answers with a partner or group. Are your answers the same or different?

	agree			disagree	
a. I admire sports stars.	1	2	3	4	5
b. Parents should force their kids to eat vegetables.	1	2	3	4	5
c. It's OK for children to take what they want.	1	2	3	4	5
d. I still discover new information about myself.	1	2	3	4	5
e. It's fun to explore your own city.	1	2	3	4	5
f. The most important explorers lived a long time ago.	1	2	3	4	5
g. Students should have admiration for their teachers.	1	2	3	4	5
h. I would like to trade jobs with someone for a day .	1	2	3	4	5
i. Trade is usually made with money, not goods or services.	1	2	3	4	5
j. Only scientists make important discoveries.	1	2	3	4	5

2. Complete the sentences. Then compare them with a partner.

   a. I <u>admire</u> people who _____.

   b. Many people think we should <u>explore</u> space because _____.

   c. Sometimes I have to <u>force</u> myself to _____.

   d. One country that the U.S. <u>trades</u> with is _____.

   e. One new food that I <u>discovered</u> recently is _____.

Read about It

Columbus Day

Christopher Columbus was an explorer. In the 15th century, Europe traded with Asia. Ships from Europe sailed* east around Africa. Columbus believed that sailing to the west, across the Atlantic Ocean, would be shorter. At that time, people did not know much about the Atlantic ocean. They did not know what was on the other side of it. Columbus asked King Ferdinand and Queen Isabella of Spain for help. They gave him three ships and 90 men. They promised that he could be governor* of any new land that he discovered. On August 3, 1492, Columbus and his men began their trip. About two months later, they saw land.

Columbus believed that he was on an island near India. People were already living there, but they were not Europeans. Columbus called them Indians. However, Columbus was actually in the Bahamas. These are islands near what is now the state of Florida. The people on the island, who called themselves

*sailed—traveled across the water by ship or boat
*governor—the leader of a state or province

"Taínos," were gentle and generous. Columbus wrote that they would make good slaves. A *slave* is someone who is forced to work without any wages. This person does not have any freedom. Columbus also wanted to govern the islands for Spain. He believed that there was a lot of gold there, which he planned to bring back to Spain. He hoped this would make him rich.

Columbus brought six of the Taínos back to Spain. He told the King and Queen about the islands and their people. Ferdinand and Isabella were pleased and admired his bravery. They called these islands the New World. They gave him 17 more ships and 1,500 men to go back. Unfortunately, his next three trips to the Bahamas were very sad for the Taínos. Columbus forced them to look for gold. There was not much gold, so Columbus and his men became extremely angry. They killed many of the Taínos. Columbus still hoped to become rich, so he took many of the Taínos by force back to Spain. There, Columbus sold them as slaves. Ferdinand and Isabella heard that Columbus was cruel and that he was selling the Taínos. They were angry at Columbus and his actions, so they arrested him.

Some people today admire Columbus. They say that he was brave because he sailed across the Atlantic, which was a large and unknown ocean. They say that he discovered and explored new land for Europe. Others do not have much admiration for Columbus. They say that Columbus killed many Taínos. He sold them as slaves. He was not brave; he was cruel.

How Do Americans Celebrate Columbus Day Today in the U.S?

The first Columbus Day celebrations in the U.S. were in 1792. Some cities today have parades. There are sales at many stores. Some states do not observe this holiday because they believe that it is wrong to celebrate Columbus. They don't call this day "Columbus Day." They call it "Indigenous People's Day." The Native Americans are *indigenous*, which means that they lived in the Americas first.

Check Your Comprehension

Read the story again. Write T for true or F for false.

1. Columbus wanted to find a shorter way to sail to Asia. _____

2. The King and Queen of Spain did not help Columbus. _____

3. Columbus thought that he had sailed to India. _____

4. The people who lived on the island called themselves Indians. _____

5. Other Europeans were already living on the island. _____

6. Columbus traveled to the island four times. _____

7. There was a lot of gold on the island. _____

8. Columbus sold the Taínos as slaves in Spain. _____

9. Everybody admires Columbus. _____

10. Today, all 50 states celebrate Columbus Day. _____

Think and Discuss

Work with a partner or group. Think about the reading. Discuss the questions.

1. Why do people celebrate Columbus Day today? Do you think it is good to celebrate this holiday? Why or why not?

2. What other explorers do you know about? Where did these people travel from and to?

3. Do you know of other countries that celebrate Columbus Day? Where?

4. Columbus Day remembers the beginning of a relationship between two cultures. When people from different cultures meet, sometimes there are problems. Sometimes, however, the two cultures together make each other stronger. What are the different cultures in your city or country? Are there problems between them? Do they make each other stronger? Explain.

5. Why do you think Columbus didn't respect the Taínos as equal human beings? Can you think of similar examples in history?

Write

Choose one of the topics, and write a paragraph of at least 5–7 sentences on a separate piece of paper.

1. What do you think that Ferdinand and Isabella wanted from Columbus? Why do you think that they changed their mind about him?

2. Why do some people think that Columbus was a good man whose actions had good results, while others think he was a bad man whose actions had bad results. What do you think? Explain.

3. One of the themes of the reading is exploration and taking control of land. In the history of your family's native country, are there examples of major explorers who left that country for other areas? Are there examples of explorers who came into the U.S. country and changed it? Explain.

★

Think about the Reading: Sacagawea

- The Missouri River is one of the longest rivers in the United States. Can you find it on a map? Where does it begin? Where does it end?

- What are some of the important rivers in your family's native country?

- What languages do the different groups of people in your family's native country speak? How about in the United States?

Practice New Vocabulary before You Read

Target Vocabulary

A. Learn the Words

Read the definitions. Notice how the words are used in the sentences.

courage (n.)—the ability to be very brave.

> *Firefighters need to have **courage** to go into a burning building.*

The adjective form is **courageous**.

> *Someone who can jump out of a plane is **courageous**.*

guide (n.)—someone who helps others know where to go or what to do; a leader.

> *When we went to India last year, we paid a **guide** at the Taj Majal to tell us about its history.*

The verb form is the same.

> *Dogs can **guide** people who cannot see.*

interpret (v.)—to translate from one language to another; to give meaning to something.

> *My mother does not speak English, so I have to **interpret** for her when she's in the U.S.*

The noun form is **interpreter**.

> *I am my mother's **interpreter** in the U.S. because I speak English, but she can only speak Japanese.*

purchase (v.)—to buy something.

> *I will need to **purchase** more food for my party.*

The noun form is the same.

> *I made several **purchases** for my party: food, paper plates, drinks, and napkins.*

valuable (adj.)—something or someone who is important; worth a lot.

> *My wedding ring is very **valuable**.*

The noun form is **value**.

> *These earrings have very little **value** because they are only plastic.*

Look at the sentences. The new words are underlined. Do the sentences make sense? Write yes if the sentence makes sense. Write no if the sentence does not make sense.

Example: This car was a big <u>purchase</u> for me. That means
it was free.   *no*

1. I have to <u>purchase</u> a plane ticket if I want to fly home
   for vacation.   _____

2. People who can <u>interpret</u> languages only know one language. _____

3. A <u>guide</u> at an art museum will probably know nothing
   about art.   _____

4. You are very <u>courageous</u> if you can work with wild animals. _____

5. Friendships can be extremely <u>valuable</u>.   _____

Now scan the reading on pages 36–37 for the target vocabulary words. You might find them more than once. Circle the words. Then compare your results with a partner.

B. Practice the Words

1. Read the sentences. Write A if you agree, D if you disagree, and X if you can't decide. Then compare your answers with a group.

   a. Everyone needs a guide when visiting a new city.   _____

   b. Only rich people make expensive purchases.   _____

   c. Moving to a new country is courageous.   _____

   d. The most valuable thing in life is money.   _____

   e. Everyone should purchase health insurance.   _____

   f. People who interpret English should be native speakers of
      English.   _____

   g. My parents guide me when I have problems.   _____

   h. It takes courage to love someone.   _____

2. Discuss these questions with a partner.

    a. Have you ever paid a <u>guide</u> to help you? When and where?

    b. What do you think it takes to be a <u>valuable</u> friend?

    c. How can people live life with <u>courage</u>?

    d. What kinds of things can you <u>purchase</u> from the grocery store?

    e. What are some different places that often hire <u>interpreters</u>?

Read about It

Who Was Sacagawea?

Christopher Columbus was from Europe. He explored part of North America. He met some people who were living there. They were Native Americans from a tribe* called the Taínos. There are hundreds of Native American tribes in North America. These tribes were the first people to live here. One famous Native American was a woman. Her name was Sacagawea. She was from the Shoshone tribe.

In 1803, the U.S. President was Thomas Jefferson. He purchased a huge amount of land from France. This land stretched from Mexico to Canada. It was called the Louisiana Purchase. It doubled the size of the U.S. Jefferson wanted to explore this new land. He also wanted to find a way for people to travel by river to the Pacific Ocean. He hired Meriwether Lewis and William Clark to do the job.

In 1804, Lewis and Clark began their two-year journey. They traveled with about 20 men. They sailed on the Missouri River. That winter, they were in North Dakota. There they met a young Native American woman. Her name was Sacagawea. She was about 15 years old. Sacagawea spoke Hidatsa and Shoshone, two Native American languages. Lewis and Clark asked her to come along and interpret for them when they met other tribes. She and her husband joined Lewis and Clark, although they knew that the trip could be dangerous.

*tribe—a group of people connected by a culture or a family

Sacagawea was the only woman in the group. It was a difficult journey.* The travelers were often wet, sick, and hungry. Sacagawea had a tiny baby and had to carry him on her back. She was strong and courageous. She was extremely valuable to the team because she knew the land and how to find food. She understood the Native Americans and their customs. Also, her baby was a sign of peace. This was extremely valuable to the team. Native American tribes that they met did not hurt them because of her baby.

Lewis and Clark needed horses to travel over the mountains. Sacagawea helped Lewis and Clark when they met the Shoshone tribe in what is now the state of Montana. Lewis and Clark were afraid that the Shoshone would kill them. However, Sacagawea found some of her family members in the tribe so the meeting was peaceful. She interpreted for Lewis and Clark and helped them to trade for horses and guides. Sacagawea continued with the team all the way to the Pacific Ocean.

The journals of Lewis and Clark do not tell us much about Sacagawea. But we know she had a lot of courage. The journey was dangerous. It was also probably very tiring to take care of her baby. Sacagawea was a valuable interpreter for Lewis and Clark. She helped them to be successful, and she guided them safely through the new land. In the year 2000, the U.S. put Sacagawea and her son on the dollar coin to honor her.

> "[The explorers] were trying to carry out a vision. A vision not just for the President or Congress, but for this entire country. Having [Sacagawea] and her baby along really reminded these men why we go out and do the things we do—why we work so hard to make life better for everybody." (Amy Mossett, Mandan/Hidatsa Tribal Historian)

*journey—a long trip

Check Your Comprehension

Read the story again. Then change the sentences to make them true.

land from France

Example: Thomas Jefferson purchased ~~France~~.

1. Jefferson wanted to find a way to travel on the Pacific Ocean.

2. Jefferson hired Sacagawea to explore the Louisiana Purchase.

3. Sacagawea was from the Taínos tribe.

4. Sacagawea spoke three Native American languages.

5. Sacagawea and her husband joined Lewis and Clark and about 20 other men and women.

6. The trip was safe and comfortable.

7. Lewis and Clark did not meet other Native Americans while they traveled.

8. Lewis and Clark interpreted for the Shoshone.

9. Sacagawea guided Lewis and Clark to North Dakota.

10. Lewis and Clark's picture is on the dollar coin because of their valuable contribution to our history.

Think and Discuss

Work with a partner or group. Think about the reading and your own ideas, and discuss the questions.

1. Why was Sacagawea a great American?

2. What do you think was the most interesting part of the journey for Sacagawea? The most difficult part? The most dangerous part?

3. Re-read the quote by Sacagawea at the end of the story. Do you agree that most people work hard to make life better for future generations?

Write

Choose one of the topics, and write a paragraph of at least 5–7 sentences on a separate sheet of paper.

1. There are more statues, rivers, lakes, and parks named after Sacagawea today than after any other woman in American history. Why do you think that Sacagawea is such an important hero to Americans?

2. Who is an important woman in the history of your family's native country? What makes her a hero?

3. Have you ever interpreted for someone? Have you ever been a guide for someone? Was it difficult? Did you feel valuable? Describe your experiences.

Complete a Project

Where Have You Traveled?

1. You are going to interview someone in English about where he or she has traveled. This could be either a vacation or a business trip. Use the form. Ask these questions.

What is your name?_____

What is your destination?_____

What language is spoken there?_____

What was the reason that you took this trip? _____

Did you enjoy your trip? Why / Why not? _____

_____

_____

_____

_____

What was the most difficult part of this trip? _____

_____

_____

_____

What was something that you learned about yourself or other people on this trip? _____

_____

_____

_____

2. Prepare a short written report for your class. Explain what you learned about the person's trip. Would you recommend this destination to your classmates? Why or why not? Write your report. Present your report to your class.

My report on an American's trip:

_____

_____

_____

_____

_____

_____

_____

_____

_____

_____

UNIT 3

Veterans Day and Jackie Cochran

Think about the Reading: Veterans Day

- Has your family's native country been at war before? When?

- What do you already know about World War I? When was it? Which countries were involved?

Practice New Vocabulary before You Read

Target Vocabulary

A. Learn the Words

Read the definitions. Notice how the words are used in the sentences.

ally (n.)—a person, group, or country that has a connection to another person, group, or country for a common goal.

> *Russia, France, and Great Britain were **allies** in World War I.* (This means that they fought together against other countries.)

The adjective form is **allied**.

> *The **allied** powers in World War I included Russia, France, and Great Britain.*

brave (adj.)—the ability to face fear or danger.

> *Soldiers in a war are very **brave**.*

The noun form is **bravery**.

> *It takes a lot of **bravery** to fight in a war.*

hero (n.)—a man or woman who does something great, generous, and courageous, usually for another person.

> *My grandfather was a **hero** in World War II because he saved another man's life.*

The adjective form is **heroic**.

> *Saving that man's life was a **heroic** thing to do.*

respect (v)—to show high value and honor for something or someone.

> *We teach our children to **respect** others. This means that we teach them to tell the truth, to be polite, and to listen well when others are speaking.*

The noun form is the same.

> *Students need to show **respect** to their teachers.*

veteran (n.)—a person who was in the armed forces and who was in active duty.

> *My grandfather was a **veteran** of World War II because he fought in that war.*

Complete the paragraph with words from the vocabulary list. Be careful! You might need to change the form of the word or the verb ending.

When countries fight wars, they sometimes group together

with other countries who are their ① _____.

This connection makes them stronger. Many women and men

must go to work in the war as soldiers. These are all

② _____ people. Several of these soldiers might

even become ③ _____. In most countries,

④ _____ of a war are treated with great

⑤ _____ for the service that they have given.

> Now scan the reading on page 44–45 for the target vocabulary words. You might find them more than once. Circle the words. Then compare your results with a partner.

B. Practice the Words

1. Read the sentences. Circle the number that reflects how much you agree or disagree. This is your opinion. Then compare your answers with a partner or group. Are your answers the same or different?

		agree		disagree		
a.	Being brave is the same as not being afraid.	1	2	3	4	5
b.	Only adults can be heroes.	1	2	3	4	5
c.	Parents should show respect to their children.	1	2	3	4	5
d.	It's important to have allies at school.	1	2	3	4	5
e.	It's easy to do heroic things.	1	2	3	4	5
f.	Everyone should respect veterans.	1	2	3	4	5
g.	It takes bravery to go to school.	1	2	3	4	5
h.	A cartoon character can be a hero.	1	2	3	4	5
i.	Allies do not have to like each other.	1	2	3	4	5
j.	I am a hero to someone.	1	2	3	4	5

2. Complete the sentences. Then compare them with a partner.

a. One way that I can <u>respect</u> my teacher is by _____.

b. A <u>hero</u> is someone who _____.

c. One job that requires <u>bravery</u> is _____.

d. One country that is an <u>ally</u> of my family's native country is _____.

e. <u>Veterans</u> are important because they _____.

Read about It

Veterans Day

Veterans Day is the day Americans remember as the end of World War I. This war took place mostly in Europe. It lasted four years. It was a deadly war. Two groups of countries fought. The Allied Powers were on one side. They included the United Kingdom, the Empire of Japan, France, Russia, Italy, and the U.S. The other group was the Central Powers. This group included the German Empire, Austria-Hungary, Bulgaria, and the Ottoman (Turkish) Empire. On November 11, 1918, the war ended. The Allied Powers had won. On this day, all of these countries signed an armistice. An *armistice* is a peace agreement.

In 1919, the President of the United States was Woodrow Wilson. He said that this important date should always be remembered. This was a day of peace. He called it Armistice Day. On this day, the U.S. should honor its soldiers.* They served, protected, and died for the U.S. They were brave heroes. Americans are proud of them.

World War II began 21 years later. This war ended in 1945. After this war, people in the U.S. wanted to change the name of Armistice Day. They wanted to honor U.S. veterans, both living and dead, who served in the armed forces.* All veterans are courageous and

*soldiers—men and women who serve in the military
*armed forces—a country's soldiers and others who participate in war

risk their lives for other people. Nine years later, after the Korean War, the
President of the United States agreed. His name was Dwight D.
Eisenhower. He changed the name of the holiday to Veterans Day.

The United States has been involved in many wars. These are the
major ones:

- The American Revolution (1775–1783)
- The War of 1812 (1812–1815)
- The Mexican War (1846–1848)
- The American Civil War (1861–1865)
- The Spanish American War (1898)
- World War I (1914–1918)
- World War II (1939–1945)
- The Korean War (1950–1953)
- The Vietnam War (1954–1975)
- The Persian Gulf War (1991)
- The War in Afghanistan (2001–present)
- The Iraq War (2003–2011)

How Do Americans Celebrate Veterans Day Today in the U.S.?

On Veterans Day, Americans show respect for U.S. soldiers. Many
people go to the cemetery. They put flags or flowers on the graves of
relatives who died in a war. A "grave" is a place where someone is buried.
Usually there is a stone or marker on this place. It often has that person's
name on it and when the person lived and died. People also put up flags
outside their homes. Many cities have parades, and famous people make
speeches.* All federal business stops for the day.

Also on this day, there is a famous ceremony in Virginia. It is at the
nation's cemetery in Arlington. Thousands of U.S. heroes are buried there.
The ceremony is at the Tomb of the Unknown Soldier. Sometimes soldiers
die in war and we don't know who they are. This monument is for them.
It's traditional for someone important to put flowers on the tomb. Everyone
there observes a moment of silence. It is a time to remember those who
died. It is a time to honor the work toward world peace.

*speeches—oral presentations to an audience

Check Your Comprehension

Read the story again. Write T for true or F for false.

1. Only two countries fought in World War I. _____

2. Veterans Day was originally called Armistice Day. _____

3. The Central Powers won World War I. _____

4. This holiday was started in order to honor U.S. soldiers. _____

5. World War I ended in 1945. _____

6. The name of the holiday was changed to Veterans Day in 1945. _____

7. The U.S. has only been involved in 12 wars. _____

8. Veterans Day is celebrated in November. _____

9. On Veterans Day today, there are parades and speeches. _____

10. Americans honor unknown soldiers on Veterans Day. _____

Think and Discuss

Work with a partner or group. Think about the reading. Discuss the questions.

1. Does your family's native country have a special day to honor veterans? What do people do on this day?

2. Are there any veterans in your family? Which war was he or she in?

3. Soldiers have to be very brave sometimes. What are some other qualities that a soldier should have? Do you know any soldiers?

4. What are some of the different jobs that soldiers might have?

5. The Tomb of the Unknown Soldier is a famous monument in the U.S. Have you ever visited a famous monument? Which one? What is one famous monument in your family's native country?

Write

Choose one of the topics, and write a paragraph of at least 5–7 sentences on a separate sheet of paper.

1. Why do countries honor veterans? Do you agree that this is important?

2. Do you think that we all need heroes in our lives? Why or why not?

3. There are many different reasons that countries fight wars. Can you give at least one reason countries fight each other?

———————————— ★ ————————————

Think about the Reading: Jackie Cochran

• What do you know about World War II? Which countries were involved?

• In your family's native country, can women work as soldiers?

• In your family's native country, are there some jobs that are just for women? Are there some jobs that are just for men? Do you think it's a good idea that some jobs are only for women and others are only for men?

Practice New Vocabulary before You Read

Target Vocabulary

A. Learn the Words

Read the definitions. Notice how the words are used in the sentences.

benefits (n.)—some kind of help or payment that a person receives. Often this is used to describe the money that people receive at their jobs to help pay for medical and retirement needs.

> *I receive **benefits** from my job, like sick leave and health insurance.*

military (n.)—the armed forces, including the Army, Navy, and Air Force.

> *One job of the **military** is to defend its country.*

pioneer (n.)—someone who is the first to do or develop something new.

> *Levi Strauss was a **pioneer** in the jeans industry because he created blue jeans.*

The verb form is the same.

> *Levi Strauss **pioneered** the idea of making pants from heavy material.*

reject (v.)—to not accept or allow something.

> *She **rejected** the job offer because they did not offer her a high enough salary.* (This means that she did not take the job offer.)

The noun form is **rejection**.

> *The company was surprised at her **rejection**. They had thought that she was going to accept their job offer.*

train (v.)—to teach, prepare, educate, or discipline someone.

> *A good football coach **trains** the team to play the sport well.*

The noun form is **trainer**.

> *A personal **trainer** at a fitness gym is someone who can teach you how to exercise and eat well.*

Choose the correct part of speech/word form for the sentence. Circle the one correct answer.

1. I am a (train / trainer). I teach people at my job how to use a computer.

2. One of the (benefit / benefits) from my job is paid vacation time.

3. The U.S. (military / militaries) has different branches, such as the Army and the Navy.

4. My three-year-old son (rejected / rejection) my offer of help. He wanted to do it by himself.

5. Gary Locke was a (pioneer / pioneers) in government because in 1997 he became the first Chinese American state governor.

Now scan the reading on pages 50–51 for the target vocabulary words. You might find them more than once. Circle the words. Then compare your results with a partner.

B. Practice the Words

1. Read the sentences. Write A if you agree, D if you disagree, and X if you can't decide. Then compare your answers with a group.

a. Good benefits are as important as good wages.   _____

b. Christopher Columbus was a pioneer in exploration.   _____

c. People should train their dogs how to behave well.   _____

d. Both men and women should work for the military.   _____

e. I sometimes reject good advice.   _____

f. Most pioneers lived a long time ago.   _____

g. The best trainers should be strict.   _____

h. Everyone experiences rejection.   _____

2. Discuss these questions with a partner.

a. What are some different benefits that a job might offer? Do you have benefits in your job? Which ones?

b. What have you trained someone to do?

c. What are some qualities that you think a pioneer might have?

d. Have you ever rejected a job offer? Explain. If not, what would make you reject a job offer?

e. What are the advantages and disadvantages of spending a lot of money on a nation's military?

Read about It

Who Was Jackie Cochran?

On Veterans Day, people remember veterans of war. One famous veteran was a very brave woman. Her name was Jackie Cochran.

Jacqueline Cochran was born in the early 1900s. Her family was very poor. She didn't go to school for many years. However, she worked hard. She loved airplanes and hoped to become a pilot some day. A *pilot* is the person who operates a ship or flies an aircraft. Jackie Cochran wanted to fly airplanes.

In 1932, Cochran got her license* to fly. She began to race airplanes. She won many awards.* In 1939, she realized that the U.S. might enter World War II. She thought that women should fly for the U.S. military. She spoke to General Hap Arnold, who was the Chief of the Army Air Forces. She said that women should be pilots, too. Women pilots could move planes from one military base* to another. This would let more male pilots fight in the war. However, the U.S. military wasn't ready for women pilots. General Arnold rejected her proposal.

But the next year, General Arnold changed his mind. He agreed with Cochran that women pilots could be a great help to the military. He knew that Great Britain was using women pilots to deliver planes to bases. Great Britain was one of the allies of the U.S. in that war. General Arnold asked her to study the women's pilot program in Great Britain. Cochran moved to England and spent some time flying for Great Britain.

*license—a permit to own, use, or operate something
*awards—prizes, certificates, or honors to celebrate excellence
*base—an area where the miitary operates

In 1942, the U.S. was in a difficult situation. Many planes needed to be moved around. However, there were not enough pilots to fly them because the male pilots were busy fighting. General Arnold asked Cochran to train women pilots in the U.S. In 1943, Cochran became the director of a new program. It was called the Women's Airforce Service Pilot program, or the WASP program. This was a non-military program, so the women did not receive any benefits or honors. However, many women wanted to join the WASP program. More than 1,000 women were trained as pilots. They began to transport planes from base to base. They also trained other pilots. By 1944, the war was ending, so the WASP program ended. However, these women were heroes. They showed the country that women could fly planes just as well and as safely as men could. In the 1970s, the U.S. military finally agreed. The military began to train women pilots. Congress also voted for an important change. They said that the women who flew with the WASPs were officially veterans. They could receive benefits.

After the war, Cochran continued to fly. In 1953, she became the first woman to fly faster than the speed of sound. She broke more distance and speed records than any other pilot, male or female. She won many awards as well as great respect for women pilots. Jackie Cochran died in 1980. In 1996, the U.S. put her picture on a postage stamp. She was honored as a pioneer of flying.

"Adventure is a state of mind—and spirit." (Jackie Cochran)

Check Your Comprehension

Read the story again. Then change the sentences to make them true.

Example: Jackie Cochran came from a ~~rich~~ *poor* family.

1. Jackie Cochran went to school for many years.

2. In 1939, women were already flying for the U.S. military.

3. Cochran wanted women pilots to fight in the war.

4. Great Britain began using women pilots after the U.S. did.

5. Cochran became the director the WASP program in England.

6. The WASP program was always part of the U.S. military.

7. The women pilots of the WASP program were immediately given good benefits.

8. The WASP program continued after World War II ended.

9. Congress voted to make the WASP pilots veterans immediately after World War II ended.

10. Jackie Cochran died after she was honored with her picture on a postage stamp.

Think and Discuss

Work with a partner or group. Think about the reading. Discuss the questions.

1. Why was Jackie Cochran a great American?

2. What is one thing that you think is especially interesting about Jackie Cochran?

3. Reread the quote by Jackie Cochran at the end of the story. What do you think she meant when she said that? Do you agree with her? Why or why not?

Write

Choose one of the topics, and write a paragraph of at least 5–7 sentences on a separate sheet of paper.

1. The postage stamp of Jackie Cochran says that she was a "pioneer pilot." Why do you think she is called that? What characteristics do you think "pioneers" have?

2. Jackie Cochran had a dream to fly, but she had many problems. She grew up very poor and did not go to school for many years. In addition, General Arnold rejected her ideas at first. However, she worked hard to make her dream come true. What is one dream that you have had in your own life? What were some of the problems that you had? How did you make your dream come true?

3. Jackie Cochran argued that women could fly as well as men. She was right, although it took 30 years for the U.S. military to agree. What are some other professional jobs (either in the U.S. or in your family's native country) that women can do now but in the past were only for men? Do you think women have achieved equality in the workplace? Why or why not?

Complete a Project

What Is Your Dream?

1. You are going to interview someone in English about a dream that he or she has in life. This dream could be educational, professional, or personal. Use the form. (<u>Note</u>: If this person's dream has already come true, change the questions to the past tense.) Ask these questions.

What is your name? _____

What is one dream in life that you have? _____

What might make this dream hard to come true? _____

_____

_____

Who or what might help you make this dream come true? _____

_____

_____

_____

Do you think that your dream will come true? When? _____

_____

_____

_____

2. Prepare a short written report for your class. Explain what you learned about the person's dream. Write your report. Present your report to your class.

My report on an American's dream:

_____

_____

_____

_____

_____

_____

_____

_____

_____

_____

UNIT 4

Thanksgiving and Squanto

Think about the Reading: Thanksgiving

- What do you know about Thanksgiving?

- What are some of your favorite foods?

- How often do you eat together with people who are from a different culture?

Practice New Vocabulary before You Read

A. Learn the Words

Read the definitions. Notice how the words are used in the sentences.

blessings (n.)—something very good that comes from God or good fortune.

> *My family is a **blessing** in my life.*

This word can also be an adjective.

> *I am **blessed** with an encouraging family.* (This means that my family is a gift in my life.)

climate (n.)—the weather in a specific location.

> *The **climate** in California is much hotter than the **climate** in Minnesota.*

poison (n.)—something that can hurt or kill when it gets inside the body.

> *Different **poisons** include some kinds of plants, chemicals, and household cleaners. It is extremely dangerous if you eat or breathe these things.*

The adjective form is **poisonous**.

> *Some kinds of mushrooms are **poisonous**. If you eat them, they can make you very sick or even die.*

season (n.)—a period of time. This is often used to talk about periods in the year with distinctive weather, like spring or summer.

> *My favorite **season** is summer because I love the warm weather!*

The adjective form is **seasonal**.

> *Some fall **seasonal** fruits in the U.S. are apples and pears.*

skill (n.)—an ability; something that is learned well.

> *My English listening **skills** are not as good as my writing **skills**.*

The adjective form is **skilled**.

> *She is very **skilled** at learning languages. This means that she can learn languages well.*

Complete the paragraph with words from the vocabulary list. Be careful! You might need to change the form of the word or the verb ending.

The ① _____ in the southwestern part of the United States is hot and dry in the summer and wet in the winter. Most people think of the southwest as only have two ② _____: cool and warm. Animals in the deserts there are ③ _____ at finding shade, food, and water. They also know very well how to stay away from ④ _____ plants and berries. Cool air or rain during hot weather is a ⑤ _____ to the people and animals who live in that part of the country.

> Now scan the readingon pages 58–59 for the target vocabulary words. You might find them more than once. Circle the words. Then compare your results with a partner.

B. Practice the Words

1. Read the sentences. Circle the number that reflects how much you agree or disagree. This is your opinion. Then compare your answers with a partner or group. Are your answers the same or different?

	agree				disagree
a. I often count my blessings.	1	2	3	4	5
b. I like the climate where I live now.	1	2	3	4	5
c. I am skilled at using a computer.	1	2	3	4	5
d. A hot, dry climate is best for everyone's health.	1	2	3	4	5
e. It's common to have some kind of poison at home.	1	2	3	4	5
f. Problems can sometimes be blessings.	1	2	3	4	5
g. My speaking skills in English are better than my listening skills.	1	2	3	4	5
h. My favorite season is the one I'm in now.	1	2	3	4	5
i. I know how to recognize poisonous plants.	1	2	3	4	5
j. Seasonal allergies are worse for me than seasonal flu.	1	2	3	4	5

2. Complete the sentences. Then compare them with a partner.

   a. The <u>climate</u> where I live now is _____.

   b. One of my <u>skills</u> is _____.

   c. _____ is <u>poisonous</u>, so parents have to put it where
      the children can't reach it.

   d. One of the <u>blessings</u> in my life is_____.

   e. My favorite <u>season</u> is _____ because _____.

Read about It

Thanksgiving

Fall is a season when people celebrate the harvest* and give thanks
for their blessings. This is a very old tradition all around the world.
However, people in the U.S. think of 1621 as the first Thanksgiving. In
that year, two very different groups of people shared a large and very
special meal. These two groups were friends. They were Pilgrims and
Native Americans.

The Pilgrims were a group of Christians from England. They did not
like the Church of England. They wanted to separate themselves from
the Church of England. In 1620, they decided to come to America.
They sailed to Massachusetts on a ship called the *Mayflower*. The trip
took 65 days. They named their new town Plymouth. Their first winter
season was very hard. They didn't know how to make the right kind of
houses for the climate in that part of the U.S. The kinds of food that
they could grow in England didn't grow well in Plymouth. More than
half of the Pilgrims died.

Luckily, the Pilgrims met some friendly Native Americans who already
spoke English. European traders and explorers had taught some of them.
However, one of the Native Americans was named Squanto. He had lived
and studied in Europe and he could speak English. He taught the Pilgrims

*harvest—the produce that farmers collect at the end of the growing season

many skills. He showed them how to grow and eat new kinds of food, like corn and clams. He taught them how to build Native American–style houses, which could protect them better in that climate.

These kinds of houses looked very different from their English-style houses. Squanto also helped them to learn about plants. He showed them which plants were poisonous and which plants could be used as medicine.

By the next fall, the Pilgrims were healthier. They were better at living in their new climate. They had a large harvest that season. They were thankful for their many blessings. They decided to have a festive meal to celebrate. They invited the Native Americans they knew. About 90 Native Americans joined the Pilgrims, bringing most of the food. For three days they all celebrated together. They ate deer, fish, beans, cornbread, pumpkin, and berries. The Pilgrims had a good relationship with the Native Americans for about 50 years. Sadly, this peace did not last. Soon more groups of European immigrants came. They forgot about this early friendship. The Native Americans and the Europeans began to fight over the land.

How Do Americans Celebrate Thanksgiving Today in the U.S.?

In 1789, George Washington made Thanksgiving a holiday. On Thanksgiving today, Americans give thanks for their blessings. People in the U.S. eat many of the same seasonal foods as the Pilgrims and the Native Americans did in 1621. They also eat turkey, stuffing,* corn, pumpkin pie, cranberry sauce, and mashed potatoes. Also on this day, many people watch football on TV. People also like to watch a very famous parade on TV. It is called the Macy's Thanksgiving Day parade. It is in New York. There are many large balloons that look like famous characters from popular culture. Some of these balloons are 60 feet tall!

*stuffing—a mixture of bread pieces, dried fruit, and vegetables

Check Your Comprehension

Read the story again. Write T for true or F for false.

1. People all over the world have the tradition of giving thanks. _____

2. The Pilgrims came to America for religious reasons. _____

3. The Pilgrims knew how to take care of themselves in their new climate. _____

4. The Pilgrims were the first English speakers in that area. _____

5. Squanto helped the Pilgrims learn how to live in that climate. _____

6. The Pilgrims learned how to build a new kind of house. _____

7. The Pilgrims and the Native Americans celebrated for 90 days. _____

8. The Native Americans and the Europeans continued their friendship for 100 years. _____

9. On Thanksgiving today, Americans celebrate George Washington. _____

10. Today, many Americans eat special food on Thanksgiving. _____

Think and Discuss

Work with a partner or group. Think about the reading. Discuss the questions.

1. Do you have a similar holiday in your family's native country? When is it? How do you celebrate it?

2. On Thanksgiving in the U.S., Americans eat many traditional foods. What are some of the traditional holiday foods (from any holiday) in your family's native country? Why do people eat those foods?

3. The Pilgrims wanted to separate themselves from the Church of England. They did not want to make the Church of England better; they wanted to start their own church. What do you think about that? Can you think of other religious groups who have separated themselves from the established religious group?

4. Squanto taught the Pilgrims many skills. Have you ever been in a situation in which you had to learn new skills? How did you learn them? Who helped you? Explain.

Write

Choose one of the topics, and write a paragraph of at least 5–7 sentences on a separate sheet of paper.

1. The Pilgrims needed to learn how to live in a different climate. The climate in Massachusetts was different from the climate in England. Compare and contrast the climate of two different places where you have lived.

2. Squanto was a good friend to the Pilgrims. He taught them many things and helped them to feel better about living in a new place. Do you know of any other person in history who has helped people get used to a new place or situation? Or, do you know any people or groups who do this today? Explain.

3. The Pilgrims enjoyed the friendship of Native Americans. Later groups of Europeans lost that friendship. What are some of the causes of the loss of friendship between groups of people? Are they similar to or different from the loss of individual friendships?

---------------------------------- ★ ----------------------------------

Think about the Reading: Squanto

- Have you ever had to do something that you didn't want to do? Describe your experience.

- Is your life different now from how you thought it might be when you were younger? How?

Practice New Vocabulary before You Read

Target Vocabulary

A. Learn the Words

Read the definitions. Notice how the words are used in the sentences.

agreement (n.)—a contract to have the same idea about something.

> *My sister and I made an **agreement** to always share our clothes with each other.*

This verb form is **agree**.

> *My sister and I **agree** about fashion, so we like to wear each other's clothes.*

fortunately (adv.)—luckily.

> *It rained today; **fortunately**, I had my umbrella with me.*

The adjective form is **fortunate**.

> *It was **fortunate** that I had my umbrella today because it rained.*

free (adj.)—not being owned or controlled by someone or something else.

> *That man will go to jail. He will not be **free** for 10 years.*

The noun form is **freedom**.

> ***Freedom** of religion is important in many countries.*

promise (v.)—to commit to do something.

> *When my wife and I got married, we **promised** to be true to each other for the rest of our lives.*

The noun form is the same.

> *My wife and I made a **promise** to always be true to each other.*

survive (v.)—to continue to live.

> *My rosebush did not **survive** the winter. It died.*

The noun form is **survival**.

> *Good weather is important to the **survival** of plants.*

Look at the sentences. The new words are underlined. Do the sentences make sense? Write yes if the sentences make sense. Write no if the sentence does not make sense.

Example: We have an <u>agreement</u>. That means we have the
same idea.   *yes*

1. I lost my wallet. <u>Fortunately</u>, I haven't found it.   _____

2. The prisoner is now <u>free</u>, so he can go home if he wants to.   _____

3. I <u>promise</u> to call you. That means I will call you if I
remember.   _____

4. The woman did not <u>survive</u> the car accident. She went
home yesterday.   _____

5. I <u>agree</u> with you about that movie. You did not like it,
but I did.   _____

Now scan the reading on pages 64–65 for the target vocabulary words. You might find them more than once. Circle the words. Then compare your results with a partner.

B. Practice the Words

1. Read the sentences. Write A if you agree, D if you disagree, and X if you can't decide. Then compare your answers with a group.

a. I agree with my best friend about religion.   _____

b. Anyone can survive a heart attack.   _____

c. Fortunately, the best things in life are free.   _____

d. Survival is the most important thing in life.   _____

e. If you promise something, you must do it.   _____

f. You must wear a seatbelt to survive a car accident. _____

g. Making a promise is easier than keeping a promise.   _____

h. All people should have freedom of speech.   _____

2. Discuss these questions with a partner.

   a. What do you <u>promise</u> to your teacher? Do you keep these <u>promises</u>?

   b. What are some <u>freedoms</u> that people in your family's native country have?

   c. What does everyone need in life to <u>survive</u>?

   d. What do you and your friends <u>agree</u> about?

   e. Do you think that you are a <u>fortunate</u> person? Why or why not?

Read about It

Who Was Squanto?

The Pilgrims came to Massachusetts in 1620 from England. When they arrived, they did not know how to survive in their new climate. One of the first Native Americans they met was Squanto. He was part of the Patuxet tribe. He helped the Pilgrims in many ways.

Squanto had met other Europeans a long time before he met the Pilgrims. When he was about 14 years old, some men from England came to explore North America. Captain* George Weymouth was the leader of the trip. When Weymouth saw the Native Americans, he was extremely interested. Weymouth did not understand the Native Americans because they looked and dressed so differently from the Europeans. He had never seen people like that before. He decided to force five of them back onto his ship. One of these was young Squanto. Weymouth took the five Native Americans back to England.

Squanto was in England for nine years. He learned English and became a skilled interpreter. The English captains promised him his freedom. In exchange, he had to first help them make a map of the coast

*Captain—the person who is leader of a ship, airplane, or train

of North America. Unfortunately, when they returned to America, Squanto was taken again. A captain named Thomas Hunt took Squanto and nearly 30 other Native Americans. Hunt put them all on his ship and brought them to Spain. He wanted to sell them as slaves. Fortunately, some religious men discovered what Hunt was doing. These men were part of a Christian community in Spain. They bought some of the Native Americans, including Squanto. These men taught the Native Americans about Christianity. They promised to help them return to North America. Squanto lived with them for four years. He finally sailed back to Massachusetts in 1618. He was a free man.

Squanto returned to his village after being gone for 14 years. Sadly, he discovered that a terrible disease* had killed his entire tribe the year before. Nobody from his tribe had survived. People today believe that this disease was either smallpox or tuberculosis. Squanto moved in with the Wampanoag tribe.

About a year later, the Pilgrims arrived. They did not know that their Plymouth was where Squanto's Patuxet tribe had been living. Squanto went to meet them, since he could speak English. He helped the Pilgrims and the Wampanoag tribe write an agreement of peace. This agreement established peace for 50 years. The two groups formed an alliance together as well. They agreed to help each other if another tribe tried to attack. Squanto stayed with the Pilgrims for two years. He was their teacher, interpreter, and guide. Squanto was still living with the Pilgrims when he died of a fever in 1622. He was not even 40 years old. The Governor of Plymouth was one of Squanto's closest friends. His name was William Bradford. He wrote about Squanto after he died. He knew that the Pilgrims had been extremely fortunate to meet Squanto. Squanto was a blessing to their lives.

> "Squanto was [the Pilgrims'] interpreter, and became a special instrument sent of God for their good, beyond their expectation." (William Bradford, Governor of Plymouth)

*disease—a serious illness

Check Your Comprehension

Read the story again. Then change the sentences to make them true.

Example:　The Pilgrims had ~~many~~ *few* skills for living in Massachusetts.

1. The Pilgrims were the first group of Europeans that Squanto met.

2. George Weymouth had seen Native Americans before he met Squanto.

3. Weymouth took Squanto and the other Native Americans to North America.

4. Squanto learned how to be a captain in England.

5. English captains took Squanto by force only one time.

6. Squanto lived with some religious men in England.

7. Squanto taught the religious men about Christianity.

8. When Squanto returned in 1618, he found that a disease had killed less than half of the members of his Patuxet tribe.

9. The Pilgrims came to live where the Wampanoag tribe was living.

10. Squanto lived with the Pilgrims for 50 years.

Think and Discuss

Work with a partner or group. Think about the reading. Discuss the questions.

1. Why was Squanto a great American?

2. How did some Europeans hurt Squanto? How did other Europeans help him?

3. Re-read the quote by William Bradford at the end of the story. What do you think he meant when he said that Squanto was "a special instrument" for the Pilgrims' good? Do you agree that Squanto was a "special instrument"? Why or why not?

Write

Choose one of the topics, and write a paragraph of at least 5–7 sentences on a separate sheet of paper.

1. One of the themes in this reading is peace. What conditions, attitudes, and actions contribute to peace between groups of people?

2. Squanto could not control where he went or what he did for many years of his life. Can you think of other people who lived in circumstances they could not control but then went on to make great achievements? Did the period when they did not have control contribute in any way? Explain.

3. Squanto suffered many horrible experiences. However, he continued to do his best, even when life was difficult. He continued to learn new skills and meet new friends wherever he went. He became one of North America's most famous historical figures. Can you think of another person who also suffered but did not give up? This could be you or someone you know. It could also be someone from world history. Explain this person's circumstances and accomplishments.

Complete a Project

How Has Life Surprised You?

1. You are going to interview someone in English about a life-changing surprise that he or she has experienced at some time. This could be about anything that has changed this person's life. Use the form. Ask these questions.

What is your name? _____

What is one life-changing surprise in your life that you did not expect to happen?

_____

_____

_____

How did this surprise change your life? _____

_____

_____

_____

Do you think this change was good for your life? Bad? Both good and bad? Explain:

_____

_____

_____

2. Prepare a short written report for your class. Explain what you learned about the person's life-changing surprise. Do you think that life-changing surprises are good for people? Not good for people? Explain your thoughts. Write your report. Present your report to your class.

My report on an American's life-changing surprise:

_____

_____

_____

_____

_____

_____

_____

_____

_____

UNIT 5

New Year's Day and Anthony Muñoz

Think about the Reading: New Year's Day

- In what month do people in your family's native country celebrate New Year's Day?

- How many days is the celebration of the New Year in your family's native country?

Practice New Vocabulary before You Read

Target Vocabulary

A. Learn the Words

Read the definitions. Notice how the words are used in the sentences.

common (adj.)—usual; ordinary.

> *Apples are a very **common** fruit in the U.S.*

debt (n.)—money or services that someone owes.

> *If you have any **debt** on your credit card, you should pay it off right away.*

prosperous (adj.)—lucky; rich.

> *My uncle is **prosperous**. He has two houses, three cars, and a boat.*

The verb form is **prosper**.

> *People who work very hard usually **prosper**.*

successful (adj.)—someone who reaches a goal; wealthy; famous.

> *My wife is a **successful** doctor because she works so hard and is very good at what she does.*

The noun form is **success**.

> *I tried to grow peppers in my vegetable garden, but I didn't have any **success**. They never grew.*

symbol (n.)—something that represents something else.

> *An eagle is a national **symbol** for many countries, such as the United States, Mexico, and Egypt.*

The verb form is **symbolize**.

> *The eagle **symbolizes** different things to different nations. For the United States, it **symbolizes** strength and freedom.*

Complete the paragraph with words from the vocabulary list. Be careful! You might need to change the form of the word or verb ending.

Credit cards can be a ① _____ of wealth in the United States. Credit cards are extremely ② _____; millions of Americans have them. If someone has a credit card, then he or she might feel ③ _____ because he or she can buy many things with the cards. The problem is that sometimes people are not ④ _____ at paying their credit card bills on time. Then they have to pay extra fees on any ⑤ _____ that they have on the credit cards. Therefore, it is very important to always pay off the whole bill each month.

Now scan the reading on pages 73–74 for the target vocabulary words. You might find them more than once. Circle the words. Then compare your results with a partner.

B. Practice the Words

1. Read the sentences. Circle the number that reflects how much you agree or disagree. This is your opinion. Then compare your answers with a partner or group. Are your answers the same or different?

	agree				disagree
a. Prosperous people are more generous than poor people.	1	2	3	4	5
b. Paying off debts is easy.	1	2	3	4	5
c. Students will have success in school if they study.	1	2	3	4	5
d. I understand common American slang.	1	2	3	4	5
e. I can draw several mathematical symbols.	1	2	3	4	5
f. Anyone can prosper.	1	2	3	4	5
g. Pizza is the most common food around the world.	1	2	3	4	5
h. Debt is always a bad thing.	1	2	3	4	5
i. Being successful is a personal choice.	1	2	3	4	5
j. I think dreams symbolize something important.	1	2	3	4	5

2. Complete the sentences. Then compare them with a partner.

a. A <u>successful</u> party has _____.

b. One <u>common</u> name in my family's native country is _____.

c. A <u>prosperous</u> person has a lot of _____.

d. I think <u>debt</u> is a good / bad thing because _____.

e. One important <u>symbol</u> in my family's native country is _____.

Read about It

New Year's Day

This is one of the oldest holidays in history. Different countries observe it on different days. It depends on the calendar. Calendars are based on the position of the sun or the moon. The most common calendar today is based on the sun. In the calendar used in the United States and many other countries, the New Year begins on the first day of January.

The New Year was first observed around 4,000 years ago in Babylon. Today that country is called Iraq. Babylonians celebrated their New

Year's Day in the spring. They believed that the spirits of the old year walked around on that day. The Babylonians wanted to scare the spirits and make them leave. Therefore, they made noise with  fireworks and whistles. Babylonians also wanted a prosperous year. They wore their best clothes, helped other people, and paid their debts on that day. They hoped that these things would bring them good luck and success in the New Year. They also made New Year's resolutions. *Resolutions* are promises to make a new start. Babylonians wanted the New Year to be better than the old one.

People in both Greece and Egypt began the tradition of using a baby as a symbol of the New Year and new life. German immigrants brought this custom to America. In the 1700s, a Scottish man wrote a song called "Auld Lang Syne." This title in his language means, "Long, long ago." People sing it on New Year's Eve. Immigrants from Europe brought this popular song to America.

How Do Americans Celebrate New Year's Day Today in the U.S.?

Americans still observe many ancient* New Year's traditions. Today celebrations begin on New Year's Eve, which is on December 31. Like the early Babylonians, many people today still believe that the first day of the new year should be special. Some people eat food that symbolizes good luck, such as black-eyed peas, cabbage, or doughnuts. There is also a tradition that began in 1907. In New York City, there is a large ball on top of a building in Times Square. At 11:59 PM, the ball begins to drop. It reaches the bottom at exactly midnight. All around the country, people make a lot of noise, and fireworks go off. They say, "Happy New Year!" They sing "Auld Lang Syne." They make a toast.* They drink champagne and kiss each other. They hope that they and their friends will prosper in the New Year. They make New Year's resolutions. Resolutions to exercise more, lose weight, or quit smoking are very common.

On New Year's Day, there are parades and college football games around the country. One famous parade in California is the Rose Bowl Parade. It has beautiful floats. *Floats* are vehicles that are covered with beautiful ornaments. These are made especially for a parade. In the Rose Bowl Parade, these floats are covered in millions of flowers. After the parade is the Rose Bowl football game. Most people in the U.S. today think of New Year's Day as a holiday to spend with friends, eat good food, and watch football on television.

Auld Lang Syne

Should auld acquaintance* be forgot
and never brought to mind?
Should auld acquaintance be forgot
and days of auld lang syne?
For auld lang syne, my dear,
for auld lang syne,
we'll take a cup of kindness yet,
for auld lang syne.

*ancient—very old
*toast—a few words of good wishes said before drinking
*acquaintance—friendships

Check Your Comprehension

Read the story again. Write T for true or F for false.

1. America was not the first country to celebrate the New Year. _____

2. The Babylonians began their New Year on the first day of January. _____

3. The Babylonians did many things to help bring a successful New Year. _____

4. Immigrants brought their New Year's traditions to America. _____

5. Most Americans celebrate on both December 31 and January 1. _____

6. Today, many Americans eat food that reminds them of the Babylonians. _____

7. The large ball in Times Square takes one minute to drop. _____

8. At midnight, people say, "Auld Lang Syne!" to each other. _____

9. Many people promise to make a better start in the New Year. _____

10. On New Year's Day today, many Americans watch football. _____

Think and Discuss

Work with a partner or group. Think about the reading and your own ideas, and discuss the questions.

1. Why don't all countries celebrate New Year's Day on the same day?

2. Is the New Year's holiday in your family's native country a major holiday or a minor holiday? How do people there celebrate it?

3. A calendar based on the position of the sun is called a solar calendar. A calendar based on the cycles of the moon is called a lunar calendar. What kind of calendar do people in your family's native country follow?

Write

Choose one of the topics, and write a paragraph of at least 5–7 sentences on a separate sheet of paper.

1. Do you think you will make any New Year's resolutions for next year? What resolutions would you like to make?

2. On New Year's Day, we think about new beginnings. Have you ever made a new beginning? Maybe this was a change in where you lived or what you studied. Maybe you changed your habits. Describe the situation.

3. The song "Auld Lang Syne" is about not forgetting old friendships. Do you think it's important to remember your oldest friendships? Why or why not? Are most of your friends old or new?

★

Think about the Reading: Anthony Muñoz

- Do you like to watch sports? Do you like to play sports? What kind of sports do you like?

- Can you name any professional sports players from any country?

Practice New Vocabulary before You Read

Target Vocabulary

A. Learn the Words

Read the definitions. Notice how the words are used in the sentences.

charity (n.)—an institution that helps people.

> *Doctors Without Borders is the name of a **charity** that works in many countries. It helps people with medical needs.*

famous (adj.)—known about by many people.

> *The Eiffel Tower is one of the most **famous** buildings in the world.*

The noun form is **fame**.

> *Most athletes achieve **fame** only after many years of hard work.*

injury (n.)—hurt or damage to someone or something.

> *A pulled muscle is a very common sports **injury**.*

The verb form is **injure**.

> *He **injured** his wrist when he fell during the soccer game.*

retire (v.)—to stop working at a profession.

> *Many people can **retire** when they are 65 years old.*

The noun form is **retirement**.

> *My grandparents spent their **retirement** traveling around the country.*

team (n.)—a group of people organized for a special purpose.

> *One baseball **team** in New York is called the New York Yankees.*

Another noun form of this word is **teammate**. It means a person who is part of a team.

> *All of the **teammates** on my daughter's soccer team wear an orange and white shirt.*

Choose the correct part of speech/word form for the sentence. Circle the one correct answer.

1. Many athletes become (famous / fame) around the world, and young people admire them.

2. It's exciting to be a part of a (team / teammate) and work with other people.

3. Many people (injury / injure) themselves at home by falling down stairs.

4. I think that (retire / retirement) will be a lot of fun.

5. Many (charity / charities) work with people whose countries are at war.

Now scan the reading on pages 79–80 for the target vocabulary words. You might find them more than once. Circle the words. Then compare your results with a partner.

B. Practice the Words

1. Read the sentences. Write A if you agree, D if you disagree, and X if you can't decide. Then compare your answers with a group.

a. A good teammate must be a good listener. _____

b. You must be rich to achieve fame. _____

c. I know how to take care of minor injuries. _____

d. I would like to be famous. _____

e. I have experience working with different charities. _____

f. Being on a sports team can be a good experience for anyone. _____

g. I would like to retire as soon as possible. _____

h. It's easy to injure yourself at home. _____

2. Discuss these questions with a partner.

a. What is one example of a <u>charity</u> that you know?

b. At what age can people in your family's native country <u>retire</u>? Do people usually stop working completely in their <u>retirement</u>?

c. What is the name of one sports <u>team</u> from your family's native country? What sport is it?

d. Who is one <u>famous</u> singer that you like? Why do you like this person?

e. What can you do if someone <u>injures</u> his or her foot?

Read about It

Who Is Anthony Muñoz?

On New Year's Day, one common tradition is to watch football. Football is a very popular sport in America. *Football* in the United States is not soccer. People around the world call this sport "American football," but Americans just call it "football." In the game of football, players move the ball by carrying it and throwing it. On New Year's Day, there are many college football games on television.

FOR YOUR
BOWL PARTY!
Bring your
favorite snack!
12:00 PM

One successful football player is Anthony Muñoz. Anthony Muñoz was born in 1958. He was born in California. He did not come from a prosperous home. Muñoz never knew his father. His mother raised him and his four brothers and sisters by herself.

Muñoz played football in college. He played offense. The opposite of the offense is the defense. Muñoz' job was to stop the players on the other team so that his teammates could try to score points. One way to score points in the game of football is to make a *touchdown*, which is worth six points. When Muñoz was in college, his dream was to play in the Rose Bowl game.

Courtesy Michigan Athletic Dept.

This is a famous game usually played on New Year's Day. Unfortunately, Muñoz seriously injured his knee at the beginning of his last year in college. However, he did not give up hope. He believed that one day he would play again. When he got out of the hospital, he began to jump rope with one leg in a cast.* He also prayed to be able to keep going and not give up. His team was good enough to play in the Rose Bowl in 1980. Muñoz' injury was better by then, and he was ready to play. He played well and even helped his teammate to score the winning touchdown. It was an exciting game: Muñoz' team won, 17–16.

After college, Muñoz played professional football for a team from Ohio. They were called the Cincinnati Bengals. Muñoz played with them for 13 years. He was very successful. He won many national awards. He also became involved in his city. He worked with several different charities.

In 1992, Muñoz retired from football. Six years later, he won the highest honor in football. He was elected to the Football Hall of Fame. The Hall of Fame honors the best professional football players in the U.S. Only 189 other football players were added to the Hall of Fame before Muñoz. Muñoz was the first player on the list who was an Hispanic American.

Muñoz has been busy in his retirement. He and his family still live in Cincinnati. Muñoz remembers that life can be difficult for kids. For that reason, he started the Anthony Muñoz Foundation in 2002. A *foundation* is an organization that helps people. His foundation helps kids' minds, bodies, and spirits. It raises millions of dollars to help children. Muñoz says that his dream is to help kids. He says that he wants to make an "impact for eternity."

> "What my success on the football field has done is give me
> a platform. God gave me a gift. Now I have to ask myself,
> 'Am I going to use my gift in a positive or negative way?'"
> (Anthony Muñoz, speaking about his reasons for starting
> his foundation)

*cast—a hard, protective bandage wrapped around a broken bone

Check Your Comprehension

Read the story again. Then change the sentences below to make them true.

Example: Americans like to watch ~~soccer~~ *football* on New Year's Day.

1. Players move the ball around in the game of football by kicking it.

2. Muñoz and his siblings were raised by his mother and father.

3. Muñoz played defense.

4. When Muñoz hurt his knee, he gave up all hope.

5. Muñoz could not play in the Rose Bowl football game in 1980.

6. Muñoz' team won the Rose Bowl football game by 17 points.

7. Muñoz played for a professional football team in California after college.

8. Muñoz still plays with the Cincinnati Bengals today.

9. The Hall of Fame honors all football players in the U.S.

10. Today, Muñoz helps other football players with the Anthony Muñoz Foundation.

Think and Discuss

Work with a partner or group. Think about the reading and your own ideas, and discuss the questions.

1. Why is Anthony Muñoz a great American?

2. How can sports be a positive experience for players? How can sports be a negative experience for players?

3. Reread the quote by Anthony Muñoz at the end of the story. Muñoz says that he has a "gift." What gift is he talking about?

Write

Choose one of the topics, and write a paragraph of at least 5–7 sentences on a separate sheet of paper.

1. Kids often look at sports players as examples for their lives. Do you think that Anthony Muñoz is a good example for kids? Why or why not?

2. Can you think of someone famous (from any country) who is a good example for kids? A bad example? Explain.

3. What is one of your gifts? How could you use your gift to help other people? How could you be a good example by developing your gift?

Complete a Project

Which Sport Do You Like?

1. You are going to interview someone in English about a sport that he or she likes. Use the form. Ask these questions.

What is your name? _____

What is one sport that you like? _____

Is this a team sport or an individual sport? _____

Do you play this sport, watch it, or both? _____

Why do you like this sport? _____

_____

_____

_____

What's the hardest part of this sport to learn? _____

_____

_____

_____

How long do you think it takes to learn this sport well? _____

_____

What is something that you don't like about this sport? _____

_____

_____

_____

2. Prepare a short written report for your class. Explain what you learned about this person's opinions about a sport. Would you recommend this sport to your classmates? Why or why not? Write your report. Present your report to your class.

My report on an American's opinion about a sport:

_____

_____

_____

_____

_____

_____

_____

_____

_____

UNIT 6

Martin Luther King, Jr.'s Birthday and Rosa Parks

Think about the Reading: Martin Luther King, Jr.'s Birthday

- What do you already know about Martin Luther King, Jr.?

- What is your race? What are the different races of people in your family's native country?

- Are people in your family's native country all treated the same by the government?

Practice New Vocabulary before You Read

Target Vocabulary

A. Learn the Words

Read the definitions. Notice the way that the words are used in the sentences.

justice (n.)—the quality of being fair.

> *The job of lawyers is to fight for **justice** for all people.*

legal (adj.)—allowed by law.

> *I don't know if it's **legal** to talk on a cell phone while I drive.*

The opposite of this is **illegal**.

> *It is **illegal** to drive while drunk.*

protest (v.)—to object strongly to something.

> *My children always **protest** when I tell them that it's time for bed.*

This word can also be a noun.

> *One common form of **protest** is to march in the streets with many other people.* (This is an organized way to make a public statement about something.)

register (v.)—to sign up to vote; to enroll in something.

> *I just **registered** to vote, so I will vote in the next election for the first time.*

The noun form is **registration**.

> ***Registration** for classes at my college will happen next week.*

support (v.)—to agree with and encourage something or someone; to vote for; to give money to.

> *I **support** our President because I agree with his ideas. I explain his actions to my family, who do not agree with his ideas.*

This word can also be a noun.

> *I always give **support** to my children, even though they are adults now. I call them on the phone and encourage them.*

Complete the paragraph with words from the vocabulary list. Be careful! You might need to change the form of the word or verb ending.

In the history of the U.S., the government did not always let all

people vote. For example, in the past, it was ① _____

for women, poor people, African Americans, and Native Americans,

to vote in the U.S. Many people ② _____ because

they believed that everyone should have the right to vote. They

believed that the U.S. should encourage ③ _____ for

all of its people. As time went on and public opinon increasingly

④ _____ the voting rights of different groups,

the U.S. government allowed these groups of people to

⑤ _____ to vote.

> Now scan the reading on pages 89–90 for the target vocabulary words. You might find them more than once. Circle the words. Then compare your results with a partner.

B. Practice the Words

1. Read the sentences. Circle the number that reflects how much you agree or disagree. This is your opinion. Then compare your answers with a partner or group. Are your answers the same or different?

	agree		disagree		
a. Everyone should support the President of the U.S.	1	2	3	4	5
b. Registering for a class is easy.	1	2	3	4	5
c. I never do anything that is illegal.	1	2	3	4	5
d. It's a lot of work to support a family.	1	2	3	4	5
e. I think protest is healthy and good for governments.	1	2	3	4	5
f. I work for justice for all kinds of people.	1	2	3	4	5
g. Everyone should be allowed to register to vote.	1	2	3	4	5
h. People should always protest when something is not fair.	1	2	3	4	5
i. My native country shows justice for all people.	1	2	3	4	5
j. It should be legal for children everywhere to drink alcohol.	1	2	3	4	5

2. Complete the sentences. Then compare them with a partner.

a. In my family's native country, it is <u>illegal</u> to _____.

b. One way that I <u>support</u> my friends is _____.

c. Only people who are _____ can <u>register</u> to vote in my family's native country.

d. People in my family's native country are currently <u>protesting</u> _____.

e. One way to show <u>justice</u> to other people is to _____.

Read about It

Martin Luther King, Jr.'s Birthday

Martin Luther King, Jr., was born in 1929. At that time in the U.S., people who were black were kept separate from people who were white. This was legal. Different races had separate schools, hospitals, and libraries. There were separate cemeteries, public restrooms, and drinking fountains. Marriage between the races was not legal. This separation of the races was called *segregation*.

King became a pastor in Alabama in 1954. A *pastor* is the leader of a Christian church. He received his Ph.D. the next year. In Alabama, African Americans did not have many rights. For example, they had to give their bus seats to people who were white. King, an African American, decided to lead a bus boycott.* He wanted to protest segregation. During the boycott, people hurt Dr. King and bombed his house. He was arrested* by the police. Many white people were extremely angry with him.

Dr. King believed in the value of all people. He continued to work for justice. After the boycott, he traveled around the world. He went to India. There, he was influenced by the life ansd work of Mahatma Gandhi. Gandhi had died about 10 years earlier. He had fought for India's independence from the British. He had not used violence. Dr. King agreed that this was the best way to bring peace.

Gandhi

When King came back to the U.S., he helped African Americans register to vote. He spoke to President John F. Kennedy about civil rights. He asked for his support.

*boycott—a way to protest by not buying or using something
*arrested—taken to jail by the police for breaking the law

In 1963, he organized a famous march. The purpose of this march was to bring national attention to civil rights. More than 200,000 people came to the Lincoln Memorial in Washington, DC. Dr. King gave a famous speech called, "I Have A Dream." Later, he began to speak about other issues. He protested the Vietnam War. He supported the work of César Chavez and workers' rights.

In 1964, Dr. King received the Nobel Peace Prize. This is a famous international award. Every year, it is given to a person or group that works for peace. That same year, Congress passed the Civil Rights Act. Segregation became illegal. The next year, Congress passed the Voting Rights Act. This made it illegal to stop people from voting. This had happened often in some parts of the U.S.

Four years later, Dr. King was in Memphis, Tennessee. While he was standing outside his hotel room, a man named James Earl Ray shot and killed him. The people of the United States were surprised and angry. People from all over the world were heartbroken for many years.

How Do Americans Celebrate
Martin Luther King, Jr.'s Birthday Today in the U.S.?

After his death, Dr. King's wife continued his fight for justice. She asked Congress to make Dr. King's birthday a national holiday. They agreed. On his birthday today, many people go to church services, speeches, or marches. This is a day of service, so many people volunteer* to help others. They remember Dr. King and how he valued all kinds of people.

> "I have a dream that my four little children will one day live in a nation where they will not be judged by the color of their skin but by the content of their character." (From the "I Have a Dream" speech, August 28, 1963)

*volunteer—to work without getting paid

Check Your Comprehension

Read the story again. Write T for true or F for false.

1. Segregation was legal in 1929. _____

2. Dr. King wanted to protest the bus boycott. _____

3. Dr. King met Mahatma Gandhi. _____

4. Gandhi taught that nonviolence was the best way to bring peace. _____

5. President Kennedy listened to Dr. King talk about civil rights. _____

6. Dr. King's famous speech was called, "I Have a Speech." _____

7. The Civil Rights Act made segregation legal. _____

8. The Voting Rights Act made it illegal to vote. _____

9. Dr. King was shot and killed in Memphis. _____

10. Today on his birthday, Americans remember Dr. King and his fight for justice. _____

Think and Discuss

Work with a partner or group. Think about the reading and your own ideas, and discuss the questions.

1. Many people today say that Dr. Martin Luther King, Jr. is their hero. What do you think makes him a hero to so many people? Why do you think some people hated Dr. King? Why do you think he was killed?

2. Dr. King worked hard to bring justice and peace to people. Who else do you know about who has worked for peace and justice? Do you know of anyone else who suffered or was killed working for social justice or peace?

3. Have you ever done something that you thought was right even when the people around you did not want you to do it? Describe your experience and how you felt.

4. Is there (or was there) discrimination in your family's native country? Explain the circumstances of the discrimination.

Write

Choose one of the topics, and write a paragraph of at least 5–7 sentences on a separate piece of paper.

1. On Martin Luther King, Jr.'s Birthday today, we think about America's history of segregation in the U.S. We think about how to live in peace with and appreciate people who are different than we are. Do you have friends who are different from you? Maybe they are a different race. Maybe they have a different religion. Maybe they are much poorer or richer than you. Do you think it's important to have friends in your life who are different from you? Why or why not?

2. Who is one of your heroes? It can be someone whom you know or someone whom you have never met. What qualities does this person have?

3. Many Americans see Martin Luther King, Jr.'s Birthday today as a day of service. They volunteer to help their community. Have you ever volunteered? Where? What was your job? What are some reasons for volunteering?

4. Look at the quote by Martin Luther King, Jr. at the end of the reading text. He talks about his dream for his children. What dream do you have for your own children? If you don't have children, then explain what dream you have for any child, in any country.

-- ★ --

Think about the Reading: Rosa Parks

- Is there anything about the social system or the government in your family's native country that you would like to change?

- Can people influence the government or make changes in your family's native country? If so, how?

- Do you feel comfortable explaining your beliefs to your family and friends? How about at school? At your job?

Practice New Vocabulary before You Read

Target Vocabulary

A. Learn the Words

Read the definitions. Notice how the words are used in the sentences.

act (n.)—something that people do; a law.

> *Jumping off the roof was a dangerous **act**! Never do that again!*

activist (n.)—someone who actively participates in changing government or social conditions.

> *Bono, lead singer for the music group U2, is a famous **activist**. He fights for human rights and the environment.*

inspire (v.)—to encourage, promote, or give good cheer to; to fill the mind with new ideas.

> *My father **inspires** me to be a better person. He is always kind to people, so I try to be kind, too.*

The noun form is **inspiration**.

> *Many poets get their **inspiration** from nature. This means that nature helps them to think of new ideas to write about.*

The adjective form is **inspirational**.

> *Dr. King's life is **inspirational** to many people. It makes people feel that they can fight for justice, too.*

refuse (v.)—to resist something; to not do something.

> *I **refuse** to buy my kids any more toys. They already have too many!*

The noun form is **refusal**.

> *My **refusal** to buy my children more toys makes them very unhappy.*

threat (n.)—a promise to hurt, punish, or kill; a sign or promise that something bad is going to happen.

> *Many families are afraid to move to some neighborhoods because of the **threat** of gangs in the area.*

The verb form is **threaten**.

> *The gang member **threatened** the young boy and said that he had to join the gang.*

Look at the sentences. The new words are underlined. Do the sentences make sense? Write yes if the sentences make sense. Write no if the sentences do not make sense.

> Example: She <u>refused</u> to buy her kids candy. She did not buy
> them candy.   *yes*

1. His <u>refusal</u> of the job offer was unexpected. I thought he wanted the job. _____

2. I don't like to listen to that music. It <u>inspires</u> me to think about beauty. _____

3. An <u>activist</u> doesn't care about anything. _____

4. She <u>threatened</u> her workers. She asked them politely to do something. _____

5. It is an <u>act</u> of kindness to hold the door open for someone. _____

Now scan the reading on pages 95–96 for the target vocabulary words. You might find them more than once. Circle the words. Then compare your results with a partner.

B. Practice the Words

1. Read the sentences. Write A if you agree, D if you disagree, and X if you can't decide. Then compare your answers with a group.

a. It's OK to refuse my family's advice. _____

b. Only famous or important people can be activists. _____

c. I'm an inspiration to someone. _____

d. Making threats is an effective way to get what you want in life. _____

e. My problems inspire me to appreciate life. _____

f. It's polite to refuse food or drink when you visit someone. _____

g. We should all do acts of kindness for strangers. _____

h. Some activists are peaceful, but some are not. _____

2. Discuss these questions with a partner.

    a. When you were a child, what did you <u>refuse</u> to do?

    b. What (or who) <u>inspires</u> you to keep learning?

    c. Do you think it's ever OK to <u>threaten</u> someone?

    d. What is one of the most dangerous <u>acts</u> that you have ever done?

    e. What is one way that an <u>activist</u> can make a difference?

Read about It

Who Was Rosa Parks?

Between 1876 and 1965, there were laws of segregation in the U.S. These laws separated the races. Rosa Parks was an African-American activist. She and others like her fought against this system.

Rosa Parks was born in Alabama in 1913. When she was about 30 years old, she began to work with a famous organization. It was called the NAACP. It is still active today. It helps to protect the civil rights of all people. Parks was the leader of the Youth Division in Montgomery, Alabama. She believed that young people were the hope for the future.

On December 1, 1955, Parks was riding home from work on the bus. Busses at that time were segregated. This meant that the African-American passengers were forced to sit in the back in what was called the "colored" section. White passengers could sit in the front. If there were no seats, blacks had to stand or get off the bus. The bus was full

Courtesy Library of Congress

that evening. Rosa Parks was sitting in the first row of seats in the colored section. A white man asked for her seat. However, Parks was tired of the injustice of segregation.

She refused to give him her seat. This act of protest was illegal. The bus driver threatened to call the police. Parks did not get up, so the police came and arrested her. They took her to jail.

The African-American community was angry about what had happened. The next Sunday morning in church, people spoke in support of Parks. Many people wanted to start a bus boycott. The African Americans of Montgomery decided to not ride the busses on Monday. Instead, they decided to walk or drive together to wherever they had to go. Martin Luther King, Jr., was the leader of the boycott. About 40,000 people chose to walk that day. The one-day boycott grew into a boycott of more than a year. For 381 days, most African Americans of Montgomery did not ride the busses. Parks became a symbol of the civil rights movement. Parks received threats. She lost her job. People threw rocks at the African Americans as they walked. Finally, the U.S. Supreme Court decided that the bus company was wrong. Segregation on busses was now illegal. The non-violent protest was successful. The bus boycott ended.

The U.S. Congress later called Rosa Parks the "Mother of the Modern-Day Civil Rights Movement." Her one act of courage seemed at first to be very small. But her refusal to accept segregation inspired the whole nation. Other cities started to protest segregation. Nine years later, all types of segregation in the U.S. became illegal.

For the rest of her life, Parks was an activist for civil rights. She received many awards and honors. She was voted one of the 100 most Influential People of the 20th Century by *Time* magazine. The country saw her as a pioneer of the Civil Rights Movement. Rosa Parks died on October 24, 2005. She continues today to be an inspiration to people around the world.

> "I have learned over the years that when one's mind is
> made up,* this diminishes* fear; knowing what must be
> done does away with* fear." (Rosa Parks)

*made up—decided
*diminishes—makes less
*does away with—erases

Check Your Comprehension

Read the story again. Then change the sentences to make them true.

Example: <u>Example</u>: Laws of segregation in the U.S. separated the ~~activists~~. *races*

1. Rosa Parks worked with the NAACP in 1913.

2. In the past, African Americans had to sit in the front of the bus.

3. On December 1, 1955, Rosa Parks was sitting in the front row of the bus.

4. That same night, Rosa Parks gave her bus seat to a white man.

5. The police arrested the bus driver.

6. About 40,000 people decided to take the busses the next Monday.

7. The Montgomery bus boycott lasted one day.

8. The U.S. Supreme Court said that the bus company had won.

9. All forms of segregation in the U.S. ended immediately after the bus boycott ended.

10. Rosa Parks stopped being an activist after the Montgomery Bus Boycott ended.

Think and Discuss

Work with a partner or group. Think about the reading. Discuss the questions.

1. Why was Rosa Parks a great American?

2. Rosa Parks was an activist for civil rights. What qualities do you think an activist might have? What is the difference between explaining your beliefs and being an activist? Are you an activist for anything?

3. Reread the quote by Rosa Parks at the end of the story. Explain what she was saying. Do you agree with her? Why or why not?

Write

Choose one of the topics, and write a paragraph of at least 5–7 sentences on a separate sheet of paper.

1. Congress called Rosa Parks the "Mother of the Modern Day Civil Rights Movement." Why do you think she is referred to as its "mother"?

2. Like Martin Luther King, Jr., Rosa Parks continues to be an inspiration to people today. Why do you think she inspires so many people?

3. Have you ever participated in a nonviolent protest? If so, what were the circumstances? What were the results? If not, would you consider participating in a nonviolent protest? For what cause?

4. Who is another activist that inspires you? This could be anyone from any country who helped bring change to a country or its government. Explain who the activist is (or was) and the change that this person helped to make.

Complete a Project

Who Is Your Hero?

1. You are going to interview someone in English about his or her hero. This person might or might not be famous. Use the form. Ask these questions.

What is your name? _____

Who is your hero? _____

What country is this hero from? _____

Why is this person your hero? _____

_____

_____

_____

How does this person inspire you? How does this person's life affect your life?

_____

_____

_____

What are some of the qualities that this person has / had? _____

_____

_____

_____

2. Prepare a short written report for your class. Explain what you learned about the person's hero. What did you find especially interesting about this person's hero? Write your report. Present your report to your class.

My report on an American's hero:

_____

_____

_____

_____

_____

_____

_____

_____

_____

UNIT 7

Saint Patrick's Day and Anne Sullivan

Think about the Reading: Saint Patrick's Day

- Look at a map. Where is Britain? Where is Ireland?

- Do people in your family's native country celebrate this holiday?

- What do you think of when you think of Ireland?

Practice New Vocabulary before You Read

Target Vocabulary

A. Learn the Words

Read the definitions. Notice how the words are used in the sentences.

associate (v.)—to be in a partnership with someone or something; to think of one thing or person when you think of another thing or person.

> *Many people **associate** food with comfort.* (This means that when they think of or eat food, they feel comforted.)

The noun form is **association**.

> *His **association** with that company prevented him from being elected.*

faith (n.)—a strong belief and trust in someone or something, usually in a spiritual being.

> *My **faith** in humanity was restored by all the people who helped after the storm.*

The adjective form is **faithful**, and it means to stay true to someone or something.

> *She was a **faithful** employee for 20 years. She always spoke well of the company and stayed there until she retired.*

legend (n.)—a story from the past that some people believe is true (or partly true) but no one is sure about.

> *Countries all over the world have different **legends** about Santa Claus.*

mission (n.)—a job or a focus that is very important.

> *My **mission** in life is to teach children. I think this is very important because children are the future. That's why I'm a teacher.*

Someone who goes to another place to work for his or her religion is called a **missionary**.

> *Buddhism was one of the first religions to send **missionaries** to other countries. In the 3ʳᵈ century BCE, these **missionaries** taught their religion to people outside of India.*

vision (n.)—a vivid, supernatural experience of seeing something; a mental image or dream; a clear idea about what should happen in the future; the ability to see.

> *Some people claim to have **visions** of events that will happen in the future.*

Complete the paragraph with words from the vocabulary list. Be careful! You might need to change the form of the word or verb ending.

Do you ① _____ religion with truth? Or do you

think that ② _____ in God is superstition and that

stories of religious founders are ③ _____. Many

people put their whole life into their religious work. Some even

become ④ _____ and leave their homes and give

up the comforts of life. They work for very little or no money or

in difficult situations. People who are not religious may find it

difficult to understand the ⑤ _____ of those who

do this kind of work. However, people of different beliefs have

been doing this for centuries.

> Now scan the reading on pages 105–106 for the target vocabulary words. You might find them more than once. Circle the words. Then compare your results with a partner.

B. Practice the Words

1. Read the sentences. Circle the number that reflects how much you agree or disagree. This is your opinion. Then compare your answers with a partner or group. Are your answers the same or different?

	agree				disagree
a. My vision is to be fluent in English.	1	2	3	4	5
b. I associate winter with snow.	1	2	3	4	5
c. Missionaries are courageous.	1	2	3	4	5
d. I enjoy reading legends from other countries.	1	2	3	4	5
e. My friends and I share the same faith.	1	2	3	4	5
f. My mission in life is to serve other people.	1	2	3	4	5
g. I associate countries with famous architecture and landmarks.	1	2	3	4	5
h. It's possible to experience supernatural visions.	1	2	3	4	5
i. My family's native country has many legends.	1	2	3	4	5
j. Boyfriends and girlfriends should be faithful to each other.	1	2	3	4	5

2. Complete the sentences. Then compare them with a partner.

a. I associate the color black with _____.

b. I am faithful to _____.

c. One famous legend that I know is about _____.

d. The mission of a police officer is to _____.

e. Martin Luther King, Jr. had a vision that _____.

Read about It

Saint Patrick's Day

Patrick's birth name was Maewyn Succat. He was born in Britain around 385 AD to Catholic parents. The Catholic Church is part of the Christian Church. When Maewyn was about 16 years old, Druids took him by force. The Druids were ruling Ireland at that time. They were not Christian, and Ireland was not a Christian country. They took Maewyn to Ireland and sold him as a slave. Maewyn had to work as a shepherd. A *shepherd* is someone who takes care of sheep. During this time, his faith grew. He finally escaped* after six years and returned home.

Both in Ireland and Britain, Maewyn had strange visions. In them, he saw a man who asked Maewyn to return to Ireland and teach the people about Christianity. Therefore, when he was in his 40s, he returned to Ireland. This time, Pope Celestine sent him. The Pope is the leader of the Catholic Church. Pope Celestine was deeply inspired by Maewyn's visions. He wanted Maewyn to have the full support of the Catholic Church. He changed Maewyn's name to Patrick. This is a Christian name.

Patrick was a missionary in Ireland for 40 years. He taught many people about Christianity. Much of Ireland became Christian. Patrick helped build churches and schools. It was difficult work. Many Druids did not want Patrick to teach the people a new religion. They beat him. They arrested him. However, Patrick stayed because he believed in his mission, and the people of

*escaped—ran away to be free

Ireland loved him. There are many famous legends about Patrick. One legend is how he explained the Christian belief about the Trinity. This is the belief that God has three parts. Patrick compared the Trinity to the shamrock plant. This is a tiny green plant found all over Ireland. It has three leaves connected to its stem. He hoped this association would help people to understand a difficult idea.

Most people believe that Patrick died on March 17. Several hundred years later, the Catholic Church made Patrick the official Saint of Ireland. A *saint* is a person who the Church believes has a special relationship with God.

How Do Americans Celebrate Saint Patrick's Day Today in the U.S.?

The U.S. has millions of Irish immigrants. On this holiday, Americans celebrate Ireland and the Irish who came to America. Everyone can have fun with this holiday, both Irish and non-Irish, Catholic and non-Catholic. In 1737, Boston had the first Saint Patrick's Day parade. Today, Boston, New York City, and Chicago have the most famous parades. Because Ireland is a very green island, many people associate Ireland with the color green. People in the U.S. wear green clothes on this holiday and eat or drink green-colored food and drinks. Chicago even puts the color green into the river that runs through the city. There are pictures of green shamrocks everywhere. One tradition says that if you are not wearing green on this day, then anyone can pinch* you.

*pinch—squeeze skin together

Check Your Comprehension

Read the story again. Write T for true or F for false.

1. Maewyn's family was Christian. _____

2. Maewyn was a Druid. _____

3. Maewyn chose to work as a shepherd. _____

4. Maewyn did not pay attention to his visions. _____

5. The Pope believed that Maewyn's visions were important. _____

6. Patrick's mission was to teach people about Christianity. _____

7. Patrick became a Saint immediately after his death. _____

8. Only Irish people celebrate Saint Patrick's Day today. _____

9. Many people associate the shamrock with Ireland. _____

10. This holiday is celebrated on the day that Patrick probably died. _____

Think and Discuss

Work with a partner or group. Think about the reading and your own ideas, and discuss the questions.

1. When he was about 16, Maewyn was taken by force. He was sold as a slave to work as a shepherd. What were some of the things that you were doing when you were 16 years old?

2. The Druids took Maewyn to Ireland by force. How did good come out of this bad situation for him?

3. Patrick was not born in Ireland. The Irish people were not his people. Yet he stayed because he believed in his mission. Do you think that it was brave or foolish of Patrick to return to Ireland? Explain your answer.

4. On Saint Patrick's Day today, Americans think about Ireland and celebrate Irish traditions. Do you have any special days in your family's native country to celebrate people from other countries or their cultures?

Write

Choose one of the topics, and write a paragraph of at least 5–7 sentences.

1. Do you think that Maewyn's visions were real? Why or why not? Do you know of other people who claim to have had visions? Describe their circumstances and the visions they said they had.

2. Why do you think that the Druids did not want Patrick to teach the Irish people about Christianity? What do you think about Patrick's mission? How are religious beliefs spread in the world today? What do you think of these methods?

3. People who believe they have a mission to be of service to others are often passionate about what they do. Religious leaders, political activists, educators, and others can all have missions. Do you feel you have a special mission in life? Is there a special contribution you would like to make to society or any change you would like to help bring about?

★

Think about the Reading: Anne Sullivan

- Do you know who Helen Keller was?

- How do you feel when you can't communicate in English?

- Do you feel like you are a product of your culture? Why or why not?

Practice New Vocabulary before You Read

Target Vocabulary

A. Learn the Words

Read the definitions. Notice how the words are used in the sentences.

disability (n.)—a physical or mental condition that restrains someone's life activities and prevents that person from doing certain things.

> *My brother has a learning **disability**. He can read and write, but it takes him extra time.*

The adjective form is **disabled**.

> *That woman is **disabled**. She uses a wheelchair because she can't move her legs.*

improve (v.)—to get better or to make something better.

> *My English is **improving** this year. I can speak and understand much better now!*

This noun form is **improvement**.

> *My English teacher is pleased with my **improvement**. He says that my English is much better this year than last year.*

limitation (n)—something that controls how much another thing is possible.

> *My small son's physical **limitations** make him very angry. He wants to do everything his older brother can do, but there are many things that he still cannot do.*

The adjective form is **limited**.

> *Because he is small, my son is **limited** in what he can do. However, when he's older, he will be as strong as his older brother.*

shocked (adj.)—surprised, confused.

> *I was **shocked** to look out the window and see snow falling. It had not snowed here for at least five years!*

The noun form is **shock**.

> *It was a **shock** to see the snow. I was not expecting to see that.*

strength (n.)—physical or mental energy; potency.

> *A firefighter must have a lot of physical **strength** because he or she must lift and carry a lot of weight.*

The verb form is **strengthen**.

> *She **strengthens** her muscles at the gym because she is a firefighter. She needs her body to be strong.*

Choose the correct part of speech/word form for the sentence. Circle the one correct answer.

1. Her vision is (limitation / limited). She cannot see very well.

2. I always try to (strength / strengthen) my relationship with my wife and children.

3. Some people are (shocked / shock) when they travel to a new country. Many things are completely different from what they expected.

4. His (disability / disabled) makes it hard for him to hear.

5. We are making several (improves / improvements) to our house. We are making our kitchen and bathroom more modern.

Now scan the reading on pages 112–13 for the target vocabulary words. You might find them more than once. Circle the words. Then compare your results with a partner.

B. Practice the Words

Read the sentences. Write A if you agree, D if you disagree, and X if you can't decide. Then compare your answers with a group.

a. Anyone can improve their job situation if they want to.   _____

b. My own limitations help me to be more patient with other people.   _____

c. Having a disability is always a bad thing.   _____

d. I like the shock of jumping into cold water.   _____

e. I have a lot of emotional strength.   _____

f. My cooking skills are limited.   _____

g. You should quit studying English if you do not see an improvement in your skills.   _____

h. Disabled people always need help from others.   _____

2. Discuss these questions with a partner.

a. How can you <u>strengthen</u> your English skills?

b. What is one thing that has <u>shocked</u> you recently?

c. What are some different kinds of <u>disabilities</u> that you can you think of?

d. What is one <u>improvement</u> you have made in your life lately?

e. What is a skill in which you are <u>limited</u>? How could you improve that skill?

Read about It

Who Was Anne Sullivan?

In the 1800s, there were many problems in Ireland. Food was very limited because of plant diseases. People were dying because of hunger. Millions of people left Ireland. Many came to the U.S. Two of these immigrants were the parents of Anne Sullivan.

Anne Sullivan was born in Massachusetts in 1866. When she was seven, she got an infection in her eyes. It made her almost completely blind.* Her mother died soon after that. Her father could not take care of her. He left her at a hospital for people who were very poor or who had mental disabilities. This was a miserable place for Sullivan. She begged to go to the Perkins School for the Blind. She wanted to leave the hospital and get an education. After four years, she was finally successful and was accepted at Perkins.

Helen Keller

Courtesy Library of Congress

While at Perkins, Sullivan had two eye operations, which improved her vision. She also learned many skills. She learned to read Braille.* This is a language for people who cannot see. They "read" by using their hands to feel different "words." She also learned the manual alphabet for people who cannot hear or see. All letters and words are signed into another person's hand. When Sullivan graduated from Perkins, she was offered a job. The parents of a six-year-old girl were looking for someone to teach their child. The child's name was Helen Keller. Helen could not hear or see.

*blind—not able to see

Sullivan went to live with the Kellers. Helen could not communicate, so she was wild and hard to control. It was difficult to teach her simple skills like eating at the table or getting dressed. Sullivan signed words into Helen's hand, but Helen did not understand. She hit her many times. She tried to escape from her. Fortunately, Sullivan refused to give up. She believed that Helen could learn to communicate. One month after she arrived, something happened. Helen and Anne Sullivan were at a water faucet. Water rushed over Helen's hand. Sullivan spelled the word w-a-t-e-r into Helen's other hand. Helen's face suddenly changed. She was shocked! For the first time, she understood that a sign had a meaning. This was a new beginning for Helen. She quickly began learning words.

Helen's improvement was quick. She left home to study at Perkins and then at Radcliffe College in Massachusetts. Anne Sullivan went with her. She signed all of the lectures into Helen's hand. After Helen graduated from Radcliffe, the two women traveled around the country. They gave speeches about their success. People were shocked and inspired to see a well-educated deaf and blind person. No one knew much about these disabilities then. The great American author, Mark Twain, called Anne Sullivan a "Miracle Worker." She was a pioneer in education. Books were written and movies were made about Anne Sullivan and Helen Keller.

Many years later, Sullivan traveled to Ireland. She realized that her emotional strength came from her Irish parents and ancestors. She had never felt limited by the expectations of other people. She did not let others tell her what she could not do. She did not associate disability with inability. Like Saint Patrick, she believed completely in her mission.

> "Keep on beginning and failing. Each time you fail, start all over again, and you will grow stronger until you have accomplished a purpose." (Anne Sullivan)

Check Your Comprehension

Read the story again. Then change the sentences below to make them true.

Massachusetts

Example: Anne Sullivan was born in ~~Ireland~~.

1. Anne Sullivan got an infection when she was young and she could not hear.

2. Sullivan enjoyed living in the hospital for poor and disabled people.

3. Sullivan went to the Perkins School for the Blind and taught many skills.

4. Helen Keller's parents hired Sullivan to teach Helen how to see and hear.

5. Helen finally understood signs six years after Sullivan came.

6. Helen was slow to learn how to communicate with signs.

7. Anne Sullivan graduated from Radcliffe College.

8. Helen Keller is known today as a "Miracle Worker."

9. Sullivan's emotional strength came from Helen Keller.

10. Sullivan believed that disabled people were not able to do anything.

Think and Discuss

Work with a partner or group. Think about the reading. Discuss the questions.

1. Why was Anne Sullivan a great American?

2. Why do you think that before she could communicate, Helen was wild and difficult to control? What do you think Helen's world was like before Anne Sullivan came?

3. Reread the quote by Anne Sullivan at the end of the story. What does she mean about failing? In your experience, has failing always been a bad thing? Explain.

Write

Choose one of the topics, and write a paragraph of at least 5–7 sentences on a separate sheet of paper.

1. Millions of people from other countries have immigrated to the United States. Many Irish people came to the U.S. in the 1800s because of hunger and diseases. What are some other reasons that people immigrate to another country?

2. Toward the end of her life, Anne traveled to Ireland. She learned about her heritage and about how much she connected with her parents' culture. What connections (good or bad) do you have with your family's native culture? How has the culture influenced you?

3. What have you taught someone else to do? Describe the situation and why it was easy or difficult? It can be something simple, like teaching a child how to tie his or her shoes. Or it can be something more complicated, like teaching someone how to drive or cook.

4. Many people have disabilities. They might be physical, learning, or mental. What are some disabilities that people have? Do you know anyone with a disability? How does it affect the person and his or her life?

Complete a Project

What Do You Know about Disabilities?

1. You are going to interview someone in English about a disability. Maybe this is a disability of someone the person you interview knows about. Use the form. Ask these questions.

What is your name? _____

What is a disability that you know about? _____

_____

Do you know someone with this disability? Do you have this disability?

_____

How often do you see people with this disability? _____

_____

How does this disability limit a person's life? _____

_____

_____

_____

What can help this person to live with these limitations? _____

_____

_____

_____

What's the best and worst part of this disability? _____

_____

_____

_____

2. Prepare a short written report for your class. Explain what you learned about this disability. Do you think that this disability limits the person's life? Do you think it adds to the person's life? Explain your thoughts. Write your report. Present your report to your class.

My report on a disability:

_____

_____

_____

_____

_____

_____

_____

_____

_____

UNIT 8

Memorial Day and Abraham Lincoln

Think about the Reading: Memorial Day

- What special person or event does your family's native country remember?

- Why do you think countries like to remember their past?

Practice New Vocabulary before You Read

Target Vocabulary

A. Learn the Words

Read the definitions. Notice how the words are used in the sentences.

bury (v.)—to put in the ground and cover with dirt; to put in a grave.

> *We **buried** my grandmother in the cemetery near our home when she died last year.*

The noun form is **burial**, and it means the act or ceremony of burying someone.

> *Many people came to my grandmother's **burial**. It was a beautiful ceremony.*

decorate (v)—to make something beautiful by adding ornaments to it.

> *My sister loves to **decorate** her bedroom walls with pictures from magazines.*

The noun form is **decoration**.

> *There were many **decorations** at the wedding, like flowers, ribbons, and candles.*

lasting (adj.)—permanent or continuing for a long time.

> *My spouse and I committed to a **lasting** relationship when we got married.*

The verb form is **last**, and it means "to continue."

> *My English class **lasts** two hours.*

recognize (v.)—to know and remember, to accept and approve of, to declare in public that something or someone is extra special.

> *When my father retired from his job, the company **recognized** his many years of employment. His boss gave him a gold watch at his retirement party, and she made a speech about his years of service.*

relative (n.)—an extended family member who is related by blood or by marriage.

> *Many of my **relatives** live near me. I have many cousins, uncles, aunts, grandparents, and in-laws.*

Complete the paragraph with words from the vocabulary list. Be careful! You might need to change the form of the word or verb ending.

People all over the world have the custom of going to a

cemetery. This is the place where they ① _____

people who die. My family and I often visit the graves of our

② _____. We clean their graves and put

③ _____ around their grave stones. We do this to

remember these special people and to ④ _____

the importance that they had in our lives. Although they do not

live with us any more, memories of them ⑤ _____

forever.

Now scan the reading on pages 123–124 for the target vocabulary words. You might find them more than once. Circle the words. Then compare your results with a partner.

B. Practice the Words

1. Read the sentences. Circle the number that reflects how much you agree or disagree. This is your opinion. Then compare your answers with a partner or group. Are your answers the same or different.

	agree				disagree
a. I enjoy taking trips with my relatives.	1	2	3	4	5
b. It's important for children to go to burials.	1	2	3	4	5
c. I'm good at making party decorations.	1	2	3	4	5
d. Lasting peace between all countries is possible.	1	2	3	4	5
e. My family's native country recognizes its veterans.	1	2	3	4	5
f. The best friendships last forever.	1	2	3	4	5
g. It's fun to decorate a new room or home.	1	2	3	4	5
h. Living with relatives is fun.	1	2	3	4	5
i. It's important to recognize other people's strengths.	1	2	3	4	5
j. Most people in my family's native country are buried when they die.	1	2	3	4	5

2. Complete the sentences. Then compare them with a partner.

   a. One of my favorite relatives is _____ because

   _____.

   b. I think the secret to lasting happiness in life is _____.

   c. Animals like to bury _____.

   d. One way that I decorate my home for a holiday is to_____.

   e. Societies recognize their sports heroes because_____.

Read about It

Memorial Day

The American Civil War ended in 1865. The North and South fought against each other. The North was called the Union Army. The South was called the Confederate Army. In April of that year, the final Southern Army surrendered.* The North had won the war. Soon after, people in different states began to decorate the graves of soldiers. This soon became a new holiday. People called it Decoration Day.

Decoration Day happened every May. Its purpose was to honor the soldiers of both the North and South. It was about bringing the North and South back together again after such a deadly war. Hundreds of thousands of soldiers from both sides died in the war. People wanted healing for the country. They wanted lasting peace between the states. On this holiday, people went to the cemetery where Civil War soldiers were buried. They decorated the graves. They cleaned the graves and put flowers and flags on them. They recognized the soldiers and their service to their country. They paid respect to their lives and deaths.

This holiday changed after World War II. It officially became known as Memorial Day. A *memorial* is something that helps us remember someone or something. This change was similar to how Armistice Day became Veterans Day. People wanted to keep the holiday but make it more general. Veterans Day had become a day to recognize both living and dead soldiers. Memorial Day, on the other hand, became a day to honor American soldiers who had died in war. It also became a day to remember family and friends who died. New York was the first state to make this a lasting holiday. On this day, there were many parades. Veterans marched. Bands played music. Famous people made speeches.

*surrendered—gave up

How Do Americans Celebrate Memorial Day Today in the U.S.?

Since ancient times, people around the world have had the custom of remembering their dead. They go to burial sites to clean and take care of their relatives' graves. Americans have this same desire to remember their dead. On Memorial Day today, Americans visit cemeteries. They put decorations on the graves where their relatives are buried. They recognize soldiers who have died for their country. There are parades in many cities. People put flags outside their homes. Government flags are at half-mast. This means that flags are only raised half-way. This is a symbol of respect for people who have died.

Memorial Day is a federal holiday. It is always on a Monday. Today, this means that many people get to enjoy a three-day weekend. This weekend is also the unofficial start of summer. Some people take short trips. Many people have picnics. People enjoy parties and barbecues. They also might watch a very famous car race. It is called the Indianapolis 500. It takes place in Indianapolis, Indiana. Cars circle a track 200 times. They race for 500 miles. The race lasts many hours! This tradition began in 1911. It was on a Memorial Day weekend. Millions of people watch this race every year.

Check Your Comprehension

Read the story again. Write T for true or F for false.

1. The Confederate Army won the American Civil War. _____

2. Decoration Day was a holiday for both the North and South. _____

3. Americans put decorations on the graves of soldiers on this holiday. _____

4. This holiday changed to Memorial Day after World War I. _____

5. Memorial Day today is a day to honor soldiers who have died in war. _____

6. Also on this holiday, people remember relatives who have died. _____

7. Flags at half-mast shows honor for people who have died. _____

8. Memorial Day today is the informal end to summer. _____

9. Many people like to do outdoor activities on this three-day weekend. _____

10. The Indianapolis 500 is a car race that lasts for 500 days. _____

Think and Discuss

Work with a partner or group. Think about the reading. Discuss the questions.

1. In your family's native country, is there a day to honor friends or family who have died? How do people observe that day?

2. Did your family's native country have a civil war? When was it? Who was fighting? Why were they fighting? What was the outcome?

3. Relatives are people who are related by blood or by marriage. Friends are people who choose one another. Are there other types of special relationships that are important? Maybe friends of your parents? Friends you only know through social networks? Friends through your religion? Name the relatives, friends, and special people who are the most important to you and say why they are important.

Write

Choose one of the topics, and write a paragraph of at least 5–7 sentences on a separate sheet of paper.

1. In the United States, many people are buried in cemeteries when they die. There is usually a burial ceremony. Others, however, choose to be cremated when they die. This means that their bodies are burned. The families can keep the ashes. They can also bury the ashes or scatter them. What do people in your family's native country do when someone dies?

2. Why do you think that people around the world have so many ceremonies around death? Why do you think that people take care of graves? What do you think about these rituals?

3. Have you ever seen a car race? What did you think about it? Have you ever seen any other kind of race? (horse, boat, dog, foot?) Describe your experience.

★

Think about the Reading: Abraham Lincoln

- Do you know who Abraham Lincoln was?

- Do you think the best leaders are also the ones whom people like? Does it matter if people like them? Why or why not?

Practice New Vocabulary before You Read

Target Vocabulary

A. Learn the Words

Read the definitions. Notice the way that the words are used in sentences.

deserve (v.)—to earn a reward; to be worthy of something.

*Students **deserve** a good grade in school when they work hard.*

endure (v)—to last a long time with a difficult situation.

*When the soccer player injured her knee, she **endured** the pain so that she could stay in the game.*

The noun form is **endurance**.

*Her **endurance** is impressive. She ran a marathon without a lot of training.*

oppose (v.)—to be against something.

> *My community **opposes** the plan to build an airport in that location.*

The noun form is **opposition**.

> *I don't think that person will become the next President because the **opposition** has better ideas about how to run the country.*

result (n.)—a consequence; something that happens because of something else.

> *If you eat less food and exercise more, the **result** will be weight loss.*

This can also be a verb.

> *The war **resulted** in thousands of deaths.*

reunite (v)—to come together, or unite, again.

> *After years of being apart, the band **reunited** for a special charity concert. People were excited to hear them play together again.*

Look at the sentences. The new words are underlined. Do the sentences make sense? Write yes if the sentences make sense. Write no if the sentences do not make sense.

Example: She had a lot of experience. She <u>deserved</u> to get
that job.   _____

1. I am a better tennis player than you are. You didn't <u>deserve</u>
   to win the match.   _____

2. The <u>result</u> of adding two and two is four.   _____

3. I think public schools should be bilingual. I <u>oppose</u> that idea.   _____

4. The two friends <u>reunited</u>. They became friends again after a
   long time.   _____

5. People in many countries have to <u>endure</u> difficult situations
   like poverty and unemployment.   _____

Now scan the reading on pages 129–130 for the target vocabulary words. You might find them more than once. Circle the words. Then compare your results with a partner.

B. Practice the Words

1. Read the sentences. Write A if you agree, D if you disagree, and X if you can't decide. Then compare your answers with a group.

    a. It's good to oppose your parents sometimes.   _____yes_____

    b. Anyone can get the results that they want in school.   _____

    c. Everyone deserves a second chance if they make a mistake.   _____

    d. I am very good at enduring pain.   _____

    e. Opposition can make me stronger.   _____

    f. Not taking good care of yourself can result in getting sick.   _____

    g. Countries that fight each other should always try to reunite
       afterward.   _____

    h. Love endures forever.   _____

2. Discuss these questions with a partner.

    a. What do you think is the best way to <u>endure</u> heartbreak?

    b. Did your parents ever <u>oppose</u> any of your ideas when you were young? Explain.

    c. Do you think that it's a good idea to <u>reunite</u> with an enemy? Why or why not?

    d. What are some <u>results</u> that you work for at your job? At school? At home?

    f. Do you think that nice people always get what they <u>deserve</u> in life? Explain.

Read about It

Who Was Abraham Lincoln?

Americans began to celebrate what is now called Memorial Day after the Civil War ended. This war changed the history of the U.S. There were two important results from this war. First, the country was reunited and did not split into two countries. Second, slaves were freed and slavery was illegal. The U.S. President at this time was Abraham Lincoln.

Abraham Lincoln was born in Indiana in 1809. His family was poor. He had less than one year of schooling. He taught himself how to read

and do math. When he was 21, he moved to Illinois. He worked as a storekeeper and an army captain. He also studied law by himself. In 1836, he became a lawyer. Lincoln opposed the spread of slavery into areas that did not already have slaves. In 1847, he became a member of Congress. In 1860, he ran for President.

The South was not happy with Lincoln and did not want him to become President. People in the South thought that he opposed slavery. The South needed slaves. Cotton was its most important industry. Slaves picked cotton and made the South rich. In 1861, Lincoln became President. By then, seven states in the South had voted to separate from the country. They said that they were independent. They called themselves the Confederacy. This resulted in the beginning of the Civil War. Four more states joined the Confederacy. These states had their own President, Jefferson Davis. The country was breaking apart.

Lincoln was not against slavery at first. The U.S. Constitution protected it. But in 1857, the U.S. Supreme Court had made a decision. It ruled that the Constitution was only for white men. Lincoln disagreed. He believed that the Declaration of Independence promised freedom to all men. In 1863, Lincoln wrote the Emancipation Proclamation. This is a famous document.* It freed the slaves. Lincoln hoped that the freed slaves would come north. This would hurt the South and help the North. He also began to let African-American men serve as soldiers. He recognized their value and strength. Later that year, Lincoln made a famous speech. It was in Gettysburg, Pennsylvania. About 50,000 soldiers had died there in a battle. He said that Americans must remember why the soldiers had died. He said that the Civil War was a war for freedom. This freedom was not just for the Union but for the entire nation.

Over time, Lincoln believed that slavery should be illegal in all the states. The country needed one law about slavery. In 1865, Congress voted to change the Constitution. It said that slavery was now illegal in every state. That March, Lincoln spoke about lasting peace. He wanted the states to be reunited. On April 9, the Confederate army surrendered. The war was over. The country had endured a deadly war.

Five days later, Lincoln was at a theater in Washington, DC. John Wilkes Booth, an actor, shot Lincoln. He hated Lincoln for freeing the slaves. Lincoln died the next morning. He was buried in a cemetery in Illinois.

> "A house divided against itself cannot stand. I believe
> this government cannot endure permanently half-slave
> and half-free." (Abraham Lincoln)

*document—piece of paper that gives legal or official information

Check Your Comprehension

Read the story again. Then change the sentences to make them true.

Example: Memorial Day began after the end of ~~World War II~~. *the Civil War*

1. One important result from the Civil War was that the country was divided.

2. Lincoln went to school for many years.

3. Lincoln always opposed slavery.

4. The South needed slaves, so they wanted Lincoln to be President.

5. There were 10 states in the Confederacy.

6. In 1857, the Supreme Court said that all men deserved freedom.

7. Lincoln freed the slaves in the North with the Emancipation Proclamation.

8. In Gettysburg, Lincoln said that the soldiers had died for freedom in the North only.

9. In 1865, Congress decided that slavery was legal in some states.

10. Lincoln was killed by a man who wanted slavery to be illegal.

Think and Discuss

Work with a partner or group. Think about the reading and your own ideas, and discuss the questions.

1. Why was Abraham Lincoln a great American?

2. Lincoln was not popular with everyone in the country, yet he was a successful president. He guided the United States through its worst period in history. What skills do you think it takes to be an effective leader? Do you think that you are (or could be) an effective leader? Why or why not?

3. Re-read the quote by Lincoln at the end of the story. Do you agree with the first sentence? Can you think of other examples of how "a house divided" cannot stand?

Write

Choose one of the topics, and write a paragraph of at least 5–7 sentences on a separate sheet of paper.

1. Abraham Lincoln grew up poor. He had very little formal education. Are you surprised that he became President? Many Americans admire him and use him as a role model. Why do you think that this is true?

2. Lincoln changed his opinion about slavery. How did he feel about it when he was a member of Congress? How did he feel about it when he wrote the Emancipation Proclamation 16 years later? Do you think it is good or bad for leaders to change their minds about issues? Explain,

3. Have you changed your mind about any issues in your own life? These issues could be social, religious, or ethical. Write about what you used to believe and why you changed your mind.

Complete a Project

Have You Reunited with Someone?

1. You are going to interview someone in English about when he or she has fixed a broken relationship. Use the form. Ask these questions.

What is your name? _____

What is the name and relationship of the person with whom you had a problem? _____

_____

_____

_____

What was the problem / fight / misunderstanding that you had with this person? _____

_____

_____

_____

_____

How long were you and this person upset with each other? _____

_____

How did you and this person fix the problem? What did you say? Did you agree to change anything in your relationship or your communication?

_____

_____

_____

_____

What was the most difficult part of the problem and / or solution?

_____

_____

_____

_____

What was something that you learned about yourself or relationships through this experience? _____

_____

_____

_____

_____

2. Prepare a short written report for your class. Explain what you learned about the person's experience. Do you think that this problem hurt the relationship? Do you think that it made the relationship stronger? Write your report. Present your report to your class.

My report on an American's relationship:

_____

_____

_____

_____

_____

_____

_____

_____

_____

UNIT 9

Independence Day and Benjamin Franklin

Think about the Reading: Independence Day

- Was your family's native country ever controlled or governed by another country?

- Did your family's native country ever govern another country?

- Do you think that it's a good idea or a bad idea for one country to control another? Why?

Practice New Vocabulary before You Read

Target Vocabulary

A. Learn the Words

Read the definitions. Notice how the words are used in the sentences.

approve (v.)—to accept something; to have a good opinion about something or someone.

> *Congress **approved** the bill. They voted to accept it.*

The noun form is **approval**.

> *The **approval** of that bill means that now it is illegal to drive while talking on a cell phone.*

defend (v.)—to protect and drive danger away; to explain and support a belief.

> *Animals **defend** themselves by fighting, running away, or pretending to be something else.*

The noun form is **defense**.

> *The teenager's **defense** of her behavior helped her parents understand why she had come home so late without calling.*

ignore (v.)—to not pay attention to something.

> *My son sometimes **ignores** me when I tell him to come inside for dinner. He does not come in.*

represent (v.)—to be a symbol of or take the place of something else; to speak for someone else.

> *Our union **represents** all of the employees at our company.*

A person who represents something or someone else is called a **representative**.

> *Several **representatives** from our union will go to the national union conference this summer.*

warn (v.)—to tell someone about a possible danger.

> *My mother **warned** me to wear sunscreen because the sun was very hot.*

The noun form is **warning**.

> *There will be a storm **warning** if a tornado comes close to our city. That will give us time to find protection.*

Complete the paragraph with words from the vocabulary list. Be careful! You might need to change the form of the word or verb ending.

Members of Congress have a difficult but interesting job. They

① _____ the interests of the people in their

districts. They speak for their people. First, they listen to what

the people want, and then they write a bill to explain and

② _____ those needs to the rest of Congress.

They hope that Congress will ③ _____ their

bills. If so, then the bills will become laws. The people in the

district pay attention to their Senators and Representatives. They

④ _____ these members of Congress that if

they ⑤ _____ the people, then the people

will not vote for them in the next elections. Do you think that

you would enjoy being a member of Congress?

Now scan the reading on pages 139–140 for the target vocabulary words. You might find them more than once. Circle the words. Then compare your results with a partner.

B. Practice the Words

1. Read the sentences. Circle the number that reflects how much you agree or disagree. This is your opinion. Then compare your answers with a partner or group. Are your answers the same or different?

		agree			disagree	
a.	It's easy for me to defend my opinions.	1	2	3	4	5
b.	I always approve of my friends' decisions.	1	2	3	4	5
c.	You should ignore people who say negative things.	1	2	3	4	5
d.	How I spend my money represents who I am.	1	2	3	4	5
e.	Teachers should warn any students who might fail class.	1	2	3	4	5
f.	I'm a good representative of my family's native country.	1	2	3	4	5
g.	I can ignore noise while I'm studying.	1	2	3	4	5
h.	Parents should give their kids a warning before they punish them.	1	2	3	4	5
i.	Exercise is the best defense against sickness.	1	2	3	4	5
j.	I like to get people's approval of my decisions.	1	2	3	4	5

2. Complete the sentences. Then compare them with a partner.

   a. When I was a child, my parents <u>warned</u> me about _____.

   b. An effective <u>representative</u> would need to be good at _____.

   c. Teenagers might <u>ignore</u> their parents if their parents ask them to _____.

   d. The <u>defense</u> on a soccer team tries to _____.

   e. Sometimes parents do not <u>approve</u> of their children's _____.

Read about It

Independence Day

In the 1600s, British citizens came to America. Over time, they created 13 colonies on the eastern coast. A *colony* is an area that is controlled by a far-away government. The people who lived there were called *colonists*. The King of England ruled them. However, by the 1760s, the colonists were frustrated.* For one thing, there were often British soldiers in the colonies. The colonists did not want them there. Also, King George III made the colonists pay high taxes. However, the colonists could not vote on how to spend those taxes. Much of the taxes paid the wages of the soldiers in the colonies. In addition, the King did not let them choose which countries they could do business with. The colonists felt that their King was ignoring their rights. He did not govern them with their interests in mind.

In 1773, angry colonists got on three British ships to protest a new tax on their tea, which came from England. They threw 342 large boxes of tea into the Boston Harbor. This protest became known as the Boston Tea Party. The next year, a group of representatives from the 13 colonies met. They wanted to defend their rights. They created the first Continental Congress. The King found out and became angry. He did not believe that the colonists deserved any rights. He sent more soldiers from England. The colonists watched for British ships. On April 18, 1775, a man rode through the towns of Massachusetts on his horse. His name was Paul Revere. He warned everyone that

*frustrated—angry because a goal or a purpose cannot be met

the British soldiers were coming. His warning allowed the colonists to prepare for war. This was the beginning of the American Revolution.

The colonists did not want England to rule them anymore. They wanted to make decisions for themselves. Congress met again. Two of the representatives were Benjamin Franklin and Thomas Jefferson. Jefferson wrote a famous document. It was called the Declaration of Independence. On July 4, 1776, Congress approved it. A month later, the representatives signed it. This was very dangerous. The King could kill them for making war against him. But the colonists ignored this. They called themselves Americans for the first time.

The country was still at war with England. But on the next Fourth of July, Americans celebrated! There were bands, parades, fireworks, and speeches. Four years later, Massachusetts became the first state to approve the new holiday. Later that same year, General George Washington won the last important battle of the war. The war ended two years later. The new United States was a free country.

How Do Americans Celebrate Independence Day Today in the U.S.?

Today, people still celebrate with parades and fireworks. In many cities, private fireworks are not legal. Because of this, there are usually public fireworks shows. The whole city can enjoy them. Families and friends spend the day at parks. They have picnics and barbecues. They watch the fireworks at night.

The Declaration of Independence is now at the National Archives Building in Washington, DC.

> "We hold these truths to be self-evident, that all men are created equal, that they are endowed* by their Creator with certain unalienable rights,* that among these are life, liberty and the pursuit* of happiness." (From the Declaration of Independence)

*endowed with—given
*unalienable rights—rights that no one can take away
*pursuit—the act of trying to look for or get something

Check Your Comprehension

Read the story again. Write T for true or F for false.

1. The colonists in the 1600s were British citizens. _____

2. The colonists felt happy to have the British soldiers in the colonies. _____

3. King George had to pay the colonists many taxes. _____

4. The colonists were frustrated that the King did not listen to them. _____

5. The Boston Tea Party was a protest, not a celebration. _____

6. The King bargained with the colonists about their rights. _____

7. The American Revolution began in 1775. _____

8. The war ended on July 4, 1776. _____

9. George Washington helped to win the war. _____

10. Americans today celebrate this holiday with fireworks, picnics, and barbecues. _____

Think and Discuss

Work with a partner or group. Think about the reading and your own ideas, and discuss the questions.

1. In 1772, one of the representatives to Congress, Samuel Adams, said that some important rights were life, liberty, freedom from oppression, and freedom of religion. Which of these rights do you think are the most important rights? Explain.

2. What are some of the rights that people in your family's native country have? Are there any rights that people in your family's native country do not have? Explain.

3. Most people in the U.S. have to pay taxes. What do taxes pay for? What is your opinion about paying taxes?

4. Read the quote from the Declaration of Independence at the end of the text. Thomas Jefferson wrote it. Explain it in your own words.

Write

Choose one of the topics, and write a paragraph of at least 5–7 sentences on a separate sheet of paper.

1. Do you celebrate on Independence Day in your family's native country? Independence from whom? When is it? How do people there celebrate?

2. Both the U.S. Civil War and the American Revolution were about independence. How was the American Revolution similar to the American Civil War? What was different about these two wars?

3. Thomas Jefferson's Declaration of Independence continues to be a powerful guide for the American people today. Do you agree with him that all people are created by God to be equal? Do you think that all people deserve to be free? Do you agree that everyone has the right to try to be happy? Explain.

★

Think about the Reading: Benjamin Franklin

- Who are some of the leaders in your current city and country? How about in your family's native country?

- Are any of the cities in your family's native country influenced by ancient European or Asian cities?

- What's the nicest city you have ever been to? What does that city have that other cities do not have?

Practice New Vocabulary before You Read

Target Vocabulary

A. Learn the Words

Read the definitions. Notice how the words are used in the sentences.

effort (n.)—hard work to get something done.

*He put a lot of **effort** into learning English.*

It can also be in the plural form if it means the individual activities.

*His **efforts** to learn English were successful.*

invent (v.)—to design or make something for the first time.

> *Levi Strauss and Jacob Davis **invented** blue jeans in 1873.*

The noun form is **invention**.

> *The **invention** of the blue jeans during the California Gold Rush continues to affect people around the world today.*

moral (adj.)—concerned with right and good ethics; instructive.

> *That story has a **moral** message. It says that you must always tell the truth, or people will not believe what you say.*

The noun form of this word is **morality**, and it means the behavior that is connected to what is good and right.

> *Some people learn their **morality** from their religion. Some people learn it from their family. Others learn it from life.*

philosophy (n.)—a set of ideas about truth and life.

> *Socrates developed an important **philosophy** of education. He asked his students questions and argued with them to help them understand ideas. He believed that this was the best way to educate students. This is called the Socratic method of education. Many teachers, lawyers, and psychologists in the U.S. use this method today.*

The noun form is **philosopher**, and it means a person who studies ideas about truth and life.

> *Socrates was a Greek **philosopher** who lived several hundred years B.C.E. His student was Plato, another famous **philosopher**. Plato wrote about how to create the best kind of government. He also wrote about the meaning of the world and people.*

The adjective form of this word is **philosophical**.

> *I enjoy having **philosophical** conversations with my friends. We talk about the meaning of life.*

politician (n.)—a person (usually elected or appointed) who works in government and public policy.

> *Some of the different **politicians** in my state include the mayor, the governor, and the members of Congress.*

Another noun form of this word is **politics**, and it means the activities that people do to govern or make decisions.

> *People around the world pay attention to American **politics**.*

Choose the correct part of speech/word form for each sentence. Circle the one correct answer.

1. Dr. King's many (effort / efforts) led to the end of racial segregation in the 1960s.

2. The (invent / invention) of the ice cream cone in the U.S. happened in the early 1900s.

3. If you want to work as a (politician / politics), you should know how to get what you want.

4. My (philosophy / philosopher) in life is to treat other people the way I would like them to treat me.

5. Many people think that it is not (moral / morality) to eat all kinds of meat.

Now scan the reading on pages 145–146 for the target vocabulary words. You might find them more than once. Circle the words. Then compare your results with a partner.

B. Practice the Words

1. Read the sentences. Write A if you agree, D if you disagree, and X if you can't decide. Then compare your answers with a group.

a. I enjoy discussing moral topics with my friends. _____

b. I put effort into being fashionable. _____

c. Politicians are usually honest. _____

d. Only a genius can invent something. _____

e. The Internet is the most important invention in history. _____

f. People today can learn a lot about life from early philosophers. _____

g. My family and I agree about politics. _____

h. My morality comes from my religion. _____

2. Discuss these questions with a partner.

   a. Do you think it's ever <u>moral</u> to tell a lie? Is it ever <u>moral</u> to cheat?

   b. What's your <u>philosophy</u> on how to be happy in life?

   c. Do you think you could be a successful <u>politician</u>? Why or why not?

   d. Have you ever <u>invented</u> a new recipe? What was it?

   e. Do you think relationships with friends take a lot of <u>effort</u>? What about with family members?

Read about It

Who Was Benjamin Franklin?

Before 1776, the colonists were proud of being British. They wanted the colonies to prosper. Their vision was to make their cities great, like the cities in England. Many people worked hard to make this happen. One of the most influential of these people was Benjamin Franklin.

Benjamin Franklin is known for many things. He worked in many different businesses. He was a writer, philosopher, and scientist. He  invented many things that people still use today. Later in life, he worked in politics.

Franklin was born in Boston in 1706. He only went to school for a few years. He moved to the city of Philadelphia at the age of 17. There, he opened a printing shop. Ten years later, he began to publish a yearly book. It was called *Poor Richard's Almanac.*

An *almanac* is a book that can include stories, puzzles, and poems. It can also have information about the weather and how to take care of your house. These books were extremely popular. In Franklin's book, he also wrote proverbs* to help people improve themselves. He became famous for them. They were philosophical and funny, and they had a moral lesson.

*proverbs—simple phrases or sayings that express basic thoughts

For the next 20 years, Franklin worked in business. He put a lot of effort into improving Philadelphia. He wanted it to be beautiful and cultured, like London. He helped to clean up its streets. He made the street lighting better. He helped start the first library because he wanted the colonists to be able to read more books and improve their minds. He helped to create the first hospital in the colonies. He organized the first fire department with firefighters who were volunteers. In 1749, he began the University of Pennsylvania.

Franklin next decided to spend his time as a scientist. He made many inventions. He invented bifocals, which are glasses that help people see both near and far. He also invented an iron stove. However, he is most famous for what he learned about electricity. He found that lightning is made of electricity. He invented the lightning rod. This is something that protects structures that are hit by lightning. Buildings, bridges, and ships still use lightning rods today.

In the 1750s, Franklin became a politician. He went to live in England. He was a representative for several of the colonies. But soon, the colonists were actively opposing their King. They wanted freedom from England. The American Revolution was beginning. Franklin came home. In 1776, he signed the Declaration of Independence. He then traveled to France and asked the French to help the colonists fight the British. They approved his request. His efforts helped the Americans win the war. He returned home in 1785. Two years later, he signed the new U.S. Constitution. Two months after that, the colony of Delaware became the country's first state.

Benjamin Franklin died three years later. The people were sad to lose such an inspirational man. More than 20,000 people came to his funeral. His face is on the $100 bill.

"An ounce of prevention is worth a pound of cure."

"A penny saved is a penny earned."

"In this world nothing is certain but death and taxes."

"There are no gains without pains."

(some of Benjamin Franklin's most famous proverbs)

Check Your Comprehension

Read the story again. Then change the sentences to make them true.

Example: The colonists were ~~American~~ British before 1776.

1. Benjamin Franklin went to school for many years.

2. Franklin became a famous writer before he opened his printing shop.

3. Franklin's almanac was published once.

4. Franklin's improvements helped make London more beautiful.

5. Franklin discovered electricity.

6. In the 1750s, Franklin defended the interests of the King to the colonists.

7. Franklin went to France before signing the Declaration of Independence.

8. The French refused to help the Americans fight the British.

9. The only famous document that Franklin signed was the Declaration of Independence.

10. Franklin was born and died in Philadelphia.

Think and Discuss

Work with a partner or group. Think about the reading and your own ideas, and discuss the questions.

1. Why was Benjamin Franklin a great American?

2. Franklin was a politician for much of his life. One of the most important things that he did was to ask France for help when the colonists needed it. In what kind of situations do you ask for help? Whom do you ask? Do you ever feel uncomfortable asking for help? Why or why not?

3. Re-read the four proverbs at the end of the text. Then choose one and explain what you think it means and what its moral lesson is.

Write

Choose one of the topics, and write a paragraph of at least 5–7 sentences on a separate piece of paper.

1. Benjamin Franklin invented many things. Many of his inventions, like bifocals and the lightning rod, are still needed and used today. What would you like someone to invent? Explain this invention and why you think people need it.

2. What is a proverb that you know? Maybe it's from your family's native country. Maybe you don't know where it's from. Explain it. Does it have a moral lesson, or does it just express a philosophical idea about life? Explain.

3. People say that Benjamin Franklin was one of several "fathers" of our nation. Why do you think that they say that? Who is one of the fathers or mothers of your family's native country? How did that person help to create the country?

Complete a Project

What's the Best Part of Independence?

1. You are going to interview someone in English about living in an independent country. Use the form. Ask these questions.

What is your name? _____

What state do you live in? _____

Where were you born? _____

Do you think much about the fact that the U.S. is an independent country? Why / Why not? _____

_____

_____

_____

What do you think is the most important right or freedom that Americans have? _____

_____

_____

_____

Why do you think that this right or freedom is so important? _____

_____

_____

_____

What are some other rights or freedoms that you are thankful for? How do they affect your daily life? _____

_____

_____

_____

_____

_____

_____

_____

2. Prepare a short written report for your class. Explain what you learned about the person's ideas about freedom. How do these freedoms affect this person's daily life? Write your report. Present your report to your class.

My report on an American's ideas about independence:

_____

_____

_____

_____

_____

_____

_____

_____

_____

Appendix

Targeted and Glossed Vocabulary

Pre-Unit

1. ancestor
2. cemetery
3. congress
4. culture
5. custom
6. federal
7. honor
8. observe
9. parade
10. tradition

*immigrants
*fireworks

Unit 1

1. bargain
2. earn
3. industry
4. union
5. wage

*factories

1. effective
2. encourage
3. extremely
4. influential
5. praise

*Great Depression
*civil rights

Unit 2

1. admire
2. discover
3. explore
4. force
5. trade

*sailed
*governor

1. courage
2. guide
3. interpret
4. purchase
5. valuable

*tribe
*journey

Unit 3

1. ally
2. brave
3. hero
4. respect
5. veteran

*soldiers
*armed forces
*speeches

1. benefits
2. military
3. pioneer
4. reject
5. train

*license
*awards
*base

Unit 4

1. blessings
2. climate
3. poison
4. season
5. skill

*harvest
*stuffing

1. agreement
2. fortunately/
   fortunate
3. freedom
4. promise
5. survive

*captain
*disease

Unit 5

1. common
2. debt
3. prosperous
4. successful
5. symbol

*ancient
*toast
*acquaintance

1. charity
2. famous
3. injury
4. retire
5. team

*cast

Unit 6

1. justice
2. legal
3. protest
4. register
5. support

*boycott
*arrested
*volunteer

1. act
2. activist
3. inspire
4. refuse
5. threat

*made up
*diminishes
*does away with

Unit 7

1. associate
2. faith
3. legend
4. mission
5. vision

*escaped

1. disability
2. improve
3. limitation
4. shocked
5. strength

*blind

Unit 8

1. bury
2. decorate
3. lasting
4. recognize
5. relative

*surrendered

1. deserve
2. endure
3. oppose
4. result
5. reunite

*document

Unit 9

1. approve
2. defend
3. ignore
4. represent
5. warn

*frustrated
*endowed
*unalienable rights
*pursuit

1. effort
2. invent
3. moral
4. philosophy
5. politicians

*proverbs

Level and Word Count

Pre-Unit	6.0 / 481	New Year's Day	5.6 / 565
		Muñoz	5.5 / 542
Labor Day	5.8 / 502		
Chavez	5.4 / 549	MLK, Jr.'s Birthday	5.6 / 552
		Rosa Parks	6.1 / 533
Columbus Day	5.2 / 503		
Sacagawea	5.5 / 550	Saint Patrick's Day	5.5 / 493
		Anne Sullivan	5.7 / 558
Veterans Day	5.4 / 513		
Cochran	5.8 / 517	Memorial Day	5.9 / 508
		Abraham Lincoln	5.8 / 527
Thanksgiving	5.4 / 520		
Squanto	5.6 / 517	Independence Day	6.0 / 544
		Benjamin Franklin	6.1 / 554